MYSTERIOUS

Marie Laveau

Voodoo Queen

And Folk Tales Along the Mississippi

MYSTERIOUS
MARIE LAVEAU
Voodoo Queen

And Folk Tales Along the Mississippi

RAYMOND J. MARTINEZ

Quaint Press
New Orleans, Louisiana

Modern compilation copyright © 2013 by Quaint Press. All rights reserved. This book or parts of it may not be reproduced, copied, or transmitted (except as permitted by sections 107 and 108 of the U.S. Copyright Law and except by reviewers for the public press), by any means including voice recordings and the copying of its digital form, without the written permission of the current publisher.

Previously published in 1956 by Hope Publications, New Orleans, Louisiana (copyright © 1956 by Raymond J. Martinez), with original illustrations from the 1956 edition. No current copyright is claimed in the original text, textual matter quoted therein, or in original illustrations. No copyright is claimed in images added to the Quaint Press edition, including portrait of Marie Laveau and sketch of Lafayette.

Published in 2013 by Quaint Press. Also available in quality ebook editions.

ISBN 978-0-61575-865-7 (pbk.)
ISBN 978-1-61027-891-1 (eBook)

QUAINT PRESS BOOKS
5860 Citrus Blvd., Box D-101
New Orleans, Louisiana 70123
www.quaintpress.com

PORTRAIT OF MARIE LAVEAU

A 1920 painting of Marie Laveau (1794–1881) by Frank
Schneider, based on an 1835 painting by George Catlin

By

RAYMOND J. MARTINEZ

Author of

STEAMBOAT DAYS ON THE MISSISSIPPI
IN THE PARISH OF ST. JOHN
THE MISER'S CUP
PIERRE GEORGE ROUSSEAU, Commanding
General of the Galleys of the Mississippi
THE STORY OF THE RIVER FRONT
THE IMMORTAL MARGARET HAUGHERY
and others

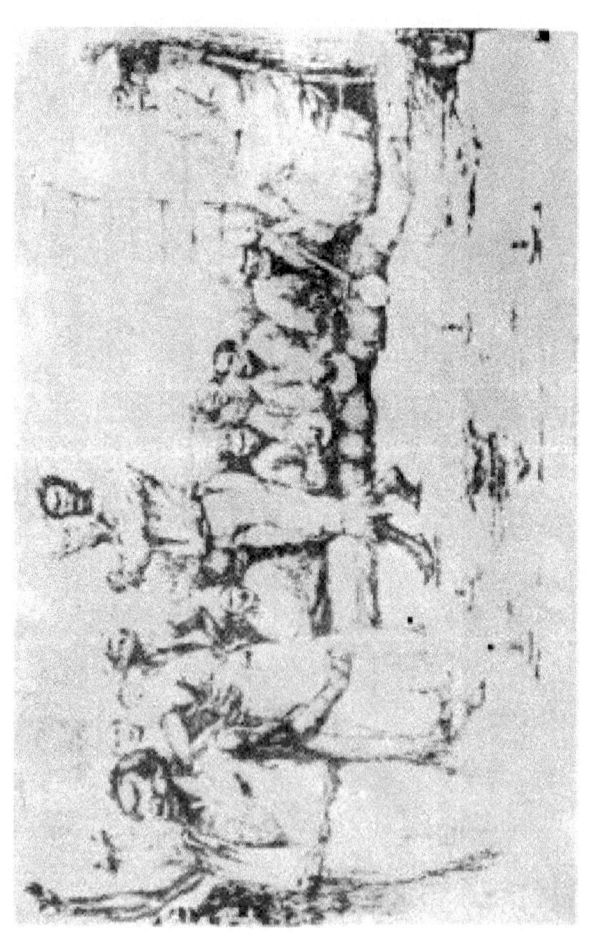

A VOODOO DANCE IN NEW ORLEANS
Century Magazine — 1886

Preface

This book is written chiefly for the reader's entertainment and amusement; it is historically correct so far as possible, but the stories of the miraculous achievements attributed to the persons involved in Voodooism are from tales handed down, and while there is much truth in them there are also some fabrications and additions which seemed necessary in order to create the atmosphere of the times; that is, to show the manner of life in the community when the greater number of inhabitants considered Voodooism and animism with much seriousness.

Folk tales, until they appear in print, are told many times, and each time in a slightly different way. Aesop's Fables all have some basis of truth, no doubt, but may have been told in a thousand different ways before they were written as they appear today. As a matter of fact, Aesop, a slave who had been freed by his master, never wrote his stories down, but they were remembered and passed on from generation to generation for more than three hundred years, when a Roman known as Babicus collected them and wrote them as they are now. Most likely some of them were lost, but it is also likely that others have been added.

The story of Marie Laveau is of interest chiefly because she succeeded in the practice of Voodooism in a community where culture was high and the Christian religion eminent. In Haiti she would have been considered a mediocre priestess, but here she was a remarkable person, who gave the people what they wanted; she mixed up Voodooism with Christianity, which was in itself a great accomplishment, for it was what no sincere Voodoo priest or priestess of Haiti could have done—or would have done, for that matter. But it was the work of a very clever person. Marie Laveau was, indeed, versatile. To some she was a saint, to others the devil incarnate.

Raymond J. Martinez
New Orleans, Louisiana,
1955

TABLE OF CONTENTS

SHE TELLS THE PEOPLE HOW TO MAKE DREAMS COME TRUE 1

MARIE LAVEAU EMBRACES THE CULT, VOODOOISM 9

TALES OF MARIE ARE AS STRANGE AS THE STORIES OF NOAH'S ARK 17

ST. JOHN'S EVE 21

THE QUEEN'S FAMOUS VASE AND OTHER FANTASTIC CLAIMS 27

DID THE MARQUIS DE LAFAYETTE VISIT MARIE LAVEAU? 31

MARIE HAD A GREAT INTEREST IN THE CONDEMNED PRISONERS 33

THE MAMMY OF THE OLD SOUTH WAS NOT A VOODOO CHARACTER 37

THE BELIEF IN ANIMISM 41

GUS ADAM, AUNT-ANN, JACK TINPAN AND OLD EVE
SAW SPIRITS FREQUENTLY 43

THE DEATH OF MARIE LAVEAU 47

THERE WERE OTHER STRANGE CHARACTERS 55

OUTWITTING THE YANKEE 59

THE BURLEY LANDING ELECTION 67

CHARLES THE GRINDER 75

GRIS GRIS ON HIS DOORSTEP DROVE HIM MAD 81

PALMISTRY IS ONE OF THE OLDEST OF PREDICTIVE SYSTEMS 87

JACK TINPAN AND THE GHOST AT HOLLINS' GATE 95

BIBLIOGRAPHY 101

MARIE LAVEAU, QUEEN OF THE VOODOOS, NEW ORLEANS

She Tells the People How to Make Dreams Come True

GLEN. *I can call spirits from the vasty deep.*
HOT. *Why, so can I, or so can any man;*
But will they come when you do call for them?

Shakespeare—Act III, *King Henry IV*

Had Marie Laveau been Glendower she could have answered Hotspur, "Yes, they come when I do call for them," and Hotspur would have believed her, just as thousands of prominent men and women of New Orleans believed whatever she said; they wanted to believe; they dared not disbelieve, for she had the power to scare the wits out of them. How she acquired this power is a subject that has never been explored. Seeing is believing, and when people were confronted with evidence that she could "make their wishes come true," and tell them what to do to bring themselves good luck, such as wearing good luck charms, usually the end of a black cat's tail or a rabbit's foot or a twig or pebble from a graveyard, or any other item, which she sold, thousands flocked to her. Why not? She was actually wonderful. She had been instrumental in causing the election of politicians to high offices; she had relieved the misery of many who had loved and lost and were pining away—suddenly there came a change and they found themselves loved in return—she had destroyed enemies or brought them bad luck; she had performed other miracles which astonished the people. How did she do this? Was it through power she gained from the help of evil and good spirits alike or was she a common sorcerer who hurt one for the benefit of another? These are questions yet unanswered.

Marie Laveau was, from all accounts, an ignorant woman. If she could read and write that was the extent of her education. It is certain that she never read a book in her lifetime, and doubtful that she ever read a newspaper. Yet men and women who had been educated at the leading colleges and universities of the United States and Europe went to seek her advice, not only in personal matters, but in matters of political activities concerning the local government and the nations of the world. There were among her clients, of course, also the lowly, who had none but personal interests, and they were in the majority.

The records of vital statistics show that Marie Laveau, free mulatto, was born at New Orleans in 1794, and married Jacques Paris, a carpenter, on August 4, 1819. The marriage was performed by Pere Antoine, who recorded the couple as free persons of color. She claimed, according to her daughter, "Mme." Alexandre, that the Laveaus were descended from the noblest blood of France. This may or may not have been true; but it was possible, of course, for it would not have been strange for a person with Marie Laveau's keen intelligence to have ancestors of more than average ability. And it was not very uncommon for French nobility to mate with "women of color."

For instance there is a strange story which the Duke of Saint Simon tells in his *Memoirs of Louis XIV and the Regency*. He says: "People were astonished this year, that while the Princess of Savoy was at Fontainebleau, just before her marriage, she was taken several times by Madame de Maintenon to a little unknown convent at Moret, where there was nothing to amuse her, and no nuns who were known. Madame de Maintenon often went there, and Monseigneur with his children sometimes; the late Queen used to go also. This awakened much curiosity and gave rise to many reports. It seems that in this convent there was a woman of color, a Moorish woman, who had been placed there very young by Bontems, valet to the King. She received the utmost care and attention, but never was shown to anybody. When the late Queen or Madame de Maintenon went, they did not always see her, but watched over her welfare. She was treated with more consideration than people the most distinguished: and herself made much of the care that was taken of her, and the mystery by which she was surrounded. Although she lived regularly, it was easy to see that she was not too contented with her position. Hearing Monseigneur[1] hunt in the forest one day, she forgot herself so far as to exclaim, 'My brother is hunting!' It was pretended that she was the daughter of the King and Queen, but that she had been hidden away on account of her color; and the report was spread that the Queen had a miscarriage. Many people believed this story; but whether it was true or not has remained an enigma."

This is not to suggest that Marie Laveau was descended from this "noble woman of color," but what happened to her nobody knows, for her whole life was shrouded with secrecy and mystery. If the noble woman of color was alive when Louis XIV died, 1715, and the Duke of Orleans became Regent of France, she would have been well around middle age. Certainly the Duke, a weak and un-

---

[1] Son of Louis XIV and Marie Therese.

scrupulous creature, with a superficial education, would not have offered her any protection, and would just as soon have sent her to the West Indies to be rid of her. All written accounts of Marie Laveau indicate that she was a mixture of Negro, Indian, and white, but this is hearsay. There is no proof. She may have been of Moorish and Spanish blood. She is always referred to as a "free mulatto," but she was born free, and it is said that her father was a wealthy white planter, and her mother was a mulatto with a strain of Indian. Yet there are others who say that her father was Charles Laveau, a mulatto, who gave her and Paris a house when they were married. Where was this white planter? The newspaper accounts do not say. (I recall that when I was a small boy my great-uncle told me that he had sat on Daniel Boone's knee. When I grew up I looked up the birth records of both and found that my great-uncle was born 20 years after Boone died). Marie Laveau's ancestry is shrouded with as much mystery as the "woman of color" at the convent of Moret.

She and Jacques Paris, who is reported to have been three-fourths white, made their residence at what is now the 1900 block of North Rampart Street, in a house which her father, Charles Laveau, gave them. They led a normal and respectable life, and although they may have attended Voodoo meetings they were not themselves practicing that cult. There was no issue from this marriage. It is said that Jacques left Marie a short time after the marriage, but this is doubtful, for she was a beautiful woman, intelligent, and capable of holding any man—if she wished to. She may have "given her husband the gate." Who knows? But it is certain that Jacques died in 1822, less than three years after the marriage, and Marie assumed the title of "Veuve (widow) Paris," which is noted in the inscription on her tomb in the St. Louis Cemetery No. 1. There is no record of the interment of Jacques Paris. If he left Marie, as some say, he may have gone back to Santo Domingo, from whence he came. The fact that there is no record of his interment, but merely the statement that he died, lends credence to the rumor that he had deserted Marie for had he died in New Orleans and while living with her there would have been a record.

Marie first began to consider Voodooism as a profession when, about 1826, she offered her services as hairdresser to the elite ladies of New Orleans. While rendering this "personal" service she found many women willing to "let their hair down," as the expression goes, and they told her of their hopes and disappointments.

For instance, she would say, "Ah, Mademoiselle, you look sad—and why?"

"Why? I will tell you why."

"You don't have to tell me; I know."

"How can you know, Marie? I've never told a soul, not even my mother."

"Yes, I know that; but you don't have to tell me; I know. It's M. Edouard. He was supposed to take Mademoiselle Regina out tonight."

"Tonight! How do you know all that?"

"I know many things, Mademoiselle, but what I know I don't say."

"She!—Regina, that scum of the earth! Her brother has a Negro mistress, black as the ace of spades, and at twenty-three he has two children. Isn't that nice? Isn't it? She's their aunt. Isn't that nice?"

"Mademoiselle, you have pretty hair."

"Don't tell me that; I wish I didn't have any at all, I wish I were dead, that's what I wish."

"You are pretty, Mademoiselle—you are good; you deserve a good man."

"I told you not to say that."

Marie twisted her body with the suppleness of a snake, then made passes in the air, and knelt at Mademoiselle's feet. "I can stop him from seeing her."

"You can stop him? What do you mean? You mean you can stop him from seeing her tonight? Is that what you mean?"

"Yes, Mademoiselle."

"How?"

"When I pass his house tonight I'll put gris gris on his doorstep, and there will be a change, a big change. You will see."

"I've heard that you can do things like that."

"Yes. That will cost you twenty-five cents—for the gris gris."

"Twenty-five cents! I'll give you five dollars if you can do it."

"Give me twenty-five cents, and if I succeed you can give me the five dollars the next time I come."

"No, I'll not do that; I'll give you the five dollars for trying—and if you succeed, Marie, I'll give you ten."

"I will succeed."

"Then hurry and fix my hair. I want you to put the gris gris on his steps right away."

Marie hurried, but she gave Mademoiselle a very beautiful hair-do, and she was pleased. She wished that Edouard could see her now.

THIS IS THE WAY YOUNGSTERS DRESSED
AND MADE LOVE IN MARIE LAVEAU'S TIME
Harper's Weekly — 1861

That night as she sat, thinking that she had made a fool of herself giving that ignorant woman five dollars for something that she could not possibly accomplish, there came a knock at the door. The valet went to answer, and returned to announce M. Edouard.

Mademoiselle's heart stood still; she nearly swooned. "Show him in." She was afraid; she did not know what had happened; she did not wish anything bad to happen to Regina, as much as she disliked her, and she wondered if M. Edouard had come to tell her bad news, something terrible which the gris gris had brought about. She did not want M. Edouard now if the gris gris had forced him to come to her, and she was cool. But his manner reassured her; he wanted her, and that was why he came. He proposed marriage that very night, and they were married in a month.

She never told him about Marie, but she went to her and, gave a good sum of money, not only for what she did, but as a bribe not to mention it ever. How did Marie do this? Mademoiselle did not ask. But Marie volunteered: "I knew it would be so; I put the gris gris. That's where it came from, from the High Heavens. Because it was right." There will follow later in this book an explanation of why Marie said that.

First, let us see how she knew that M. Edouard was not to see Mademoiselle Regina that night.

Telepathy, whose limits no one can define at present, can filch knowledge subliminally and systematically from living people at pleasure. So says Dr. James H. Hyslop, formerly Professor of Ethics in Columbia University in his book *Physical Research and the Resurrection*. "There are growing signs that a new world of facts promises to open to human vision and interest, and only self-complacent dogmatists any longer ridicule the subject." Telepathy is not a new experience or idea; it was known to the ancients. It is reported that when Caesar was in Gaul with his army a rumor was circulated in Rome that on a certain date, five weeks hence, he would arrive with 3000 prisoners he had captured. The people were jubilant. The Senate began to make preparations for a welcome, and a Roman Holiday gave rise to wonder among the inhabitants of Mars as to what was happening on the little planet called the earth. But there was a member of the Roman Senate, such as we have in Washington, who liked to investigate everything, and he recommended that a committee be appointed to inquire where this news originated. Nobody could tell. Nobody knew. It would have been impossible for Caesar to have communicated this news to Rome within a day. The swiftest messenger could not have made the trip inside of three weeks. An old woman, like Marie Laveau, had received the message via telepathy, and had told somebody who spread the news. When she heard of the Senate's purpose to investigate she either killed herself or fled the country. She may have gone to Greece and lived under another name, forever in fear. The Senate's committee reported that the rumor was a pure falsehood. But on the date specified Caesar arrived with his 3000 prisoners. Rome was amazed. The Senate appointed a second committee to investigate the first.

Marie Laveau knew nothing of mental telepathy. If her mind instantly communicated with M. Edouard's and she read his thoughts—that he had made up his mind to marry Mademoiselle—she attributed the flash of knowledge to the High Heavens or to the gris gris. The truth is that somehow, she knew not how, she became suddenly aware of what M. Edouard was going to do.

She could have gambled in her foretelling and in her promises, and taken the chance that she would win. But her average of winnings was too high. She must have had some means of knowing.

A TYPICAL VOODOO IN NEW ORLEANS
Century Magazine — 1886

Marie Laveau Embraces the Cult, Voodooism

Marie Laveau became so popular among the young ladies of New Orleans, and the money which she received for her favors was so great an amount that she felt she could do even better in a professional way. She knew that Voodooism had become the rage of New Orleans. But she also knew that the Voodoos were devil worshippers, inclined to do harm rather than good. She was too clever to accept a cult in which there was only destruction, and no profit. Anyway, as she was aware, "The devil can cite Scripture for his purpose." She proceeded to change the very purpose of Voodooism; it was to become a profitable business which offered to satisfy the desires of the people; that is, to show them how to procure the things dearest to their hearts, and for which they had long prayed. In this she was to succeed as no Voodoo Queen ever had. She was to keep the ritual, for showmanship was necessary. She knew that. There were to be the monster serpent lodging in the Alabaster box, the black cat and the rooster. Where she procured the Alabaster box is unknown. Some said that it was given her by Mommer, the chief deity of the religion, while she was still in the Congo. Other versions had it that the box was brought from Heaven. The great Zombi (as the snake was called) fed only upon fair and tender children. Serious mention of this was made in the Picayune of June 25, 1873. But Marie added to this unholy arrangement statues of saints, incense, and holy water.

These additions were the secrets of Marie Laveau's success; they were the media through which she wielded her power and authority. She used the same methods that Billy Graham is using today. It cannot be conceived that 14,500 of Scotland's people, proud of their staunch and unemotional character, would have rushed to hear him the first night of his arrival had he claimed that he as an individual brought them a message—his own message—he brought them a message of God. That is what they went to hear; what had been revealed to him or his interpretation of what was expected of the Highest of Powers. So it was with Billy Sunday, Gypsy Smith, and other successful evangelists.

There were several Voodoo queens complacently occupying their thrones when Marie decided that she was to reign alone. This precipitated a terrible battle for supremacy, nearly as bad as the War of the Spanish Succession, which lasted for several years. Marie conquered by fair means and foul. The former queens, now humbled, served under her. They had actually been subdued by her success, for she had among her clients many of the elite ladies of the city, for she knew them well (she had been their hairdresser), and there were gentlemen of prominent families who visited her. These gentlemen customarily had mulatto "mistresses" and mulatto children. Marie knew all about this, for these "mistresses" often consulted her. Obviously her claim to power did not come only from holy water and incense, but from an inside knowledge of the lives of certain ladies and gentlemen.

The Picayune of June 25, 1873 says that there were (at that time) three hundred Voodoos in the city, presided over by a queen, "and amongst whom are numbered, strange to relate, at least eight or ten white women who partake as the others in the hellish orgies. Outside of these 'firm ones' there are about a thousand more who, while ashamed to openly acknowledge their belief, secretly have faith, and can be found on the sly practicing its tenets. The belief is one of fear...."

Marie formed a liaison with Captain Christophe Duminy Glapion about 1826. Since she did not marry him the date of their coming together is uncertain. She was then 32 years old, and more attractive than when she married Paris. Glapion was 37, and was also a free person of color. He was, it is said, a very handsome man. From this union, such as it was, there were fifteen children. He died on June 26, 1855, and was buried in the Laveau tomb in the St. Louis Cemetery No. 1. He was apparently a good man, and undoubtedly a good husband.

Glapion seems to have taken no part in the Voodoo rituals, for his name is never mentioned in the newspaper accounts of that cult. Why Marie did not make a god of him instead of the snake, Zombi, is somewhat surprising, for he rendered meritorious services in the War of 1812, having been a member of the Company of Men of San Domingo at the Battle of New Orleans.[2] She knew

---

[2] During the bloody revolutionary and slave revolts in San Domingo, which began in 1791, many free mulattoes and white people fled to Louisiana. Previously the free colored people of San Domingo (numbering about 30,000) had no voice in the Government, but in 1790 had been given full citizenship. To this the whites objected and when the decree was reversed the mulattoes fled to arms, and the struggle between them and the whites gave the slaves the opportunity to revolt. There followed the bloodiest revolution in the history of the country, from which came the independence of the island in 1801. Taking a prominent part in this affair was a General Laveaux—on the side of the French.

better than to do so, for he was in the United States. Her wisdom is explained by Mark Twain, who said that Lono was a favorite god of the Island of Hawaii, "a great king who had been deified for meritorious services—just our own fashion of rewarding heroes, with the difference that we would have made him a postmaster instead of a god." Apparently Glapion was satisfied to operate behind the scenes; he may have been the bookkeeper and cashier, who handled the money which came in great quantities.

Marie had by this time become quite famous. People went out of their way for a glimpse of her, for she was the great Voodoo Queen who could do wonders in good and bad; the greatest interest was, of course, in the bad things she could do; but any bad thing she did for one was good for another.

"Sweet are the uses of adversity,
Which like the toad, ugly and venomous,
Wears yet a precious jewel in his head;
And this our life, exempt from public haunt,
Finds tongues in trees, books in the running brooks,
Sermons in stones, and good in every thing."

This was her philosophy. When the parents of a very attractive young lady offered her a good sum of money to bring about their daughter's marriage to a wealthy Creole who had spent his youth in dissipation, and had no respect for women, she agreed to the bargain and succeeded. It is said that she got a mockingbird drunk and placed it in a cage outside the young lady's window. As the bird began to sing her heart went out to the wealthy Creole. But the mockingbird was never the same after that; it became a confirmed alcoholic, and had to be fed whiskey every day. The Creole led his wife a miserable life; like the mockingbird he became a confirmed drunkard, and was finally killed in a street brawl. His wife died shortly afterwards, and her parents inherited a good sum of money. These were the "sweet uses" Marie made of adversity, and the good she found in everything.

There was a young man of a very aristocratic family in New Orleans who had seriously "wronged" a beautiful and innocent girl of a lower but respectable social station. Her father had gone to the district attorney and charged him with rape, and the evidence which he produced was very convincing. The young man's father was greatly alarmed, for public sentiment seemed strongly in favor of the young lady, owing, no doubt, to her beauty and good reputation. Moreover, the attorney employed to defend his son seemed discouraged, and talked of settling for a light sentence. Finally, the young man, being informed of his predicament, went himself to see Marie Laveau, and pleaded for help on his bended knees. He offered her a good sum of money, which, he said, he was certain his father would provide. After hearing his story, which he related in great detail, she assured him that she would bring about his acquittal.

As the time for the trial approached the young man informed his father of his interview with Marie, and of his promise.

"Ha," said his father, "that is ridiculous. But if she succeeds I will give her the house that I own on St. Ann Street."

"I will tell her that, and she will hold you to it," said the young man.

"Very well, I always keep my word."

On the day of the trial Marie made a condiment of vegetables having an agreeable odor, and placed it carefully in the right hand corner of the judge's desk. This she did about six o'clock in the morning when there were few persons about, and certainly none in the courthouse. She then placed a bag of powdered brick on the front steps of his residence, and on his front door she pinned a note which said: "The boy is innocent," and to this she had the effrontery to sign her name, believing that her influence would have weight.

The jury was composed of the playboy type of men, most of whom had probably committed the same character of crime, but had not been brought to justice. The prosecuting attorney, was, however, a man who had risen from the ranks and knew the "wronged" girl very well. He, therefore, fought hard for conviction. "Mark well what I say," he cried; "if this man is set free, then none of our young girls are safe in this city, and that would be an unusual situation in this civilized world, for the laws and customs protecting women are ancient. Read your Bible." Marie wanted to speak. She had something in her mind. But she dared not. Instead, she flipped a small ball of paper, in which was wrapped a strand of her hair, up into the air, and it fell upon the prosecuting attorney's shoulder. He said no more, but left the matter to the jury.

The verdict rendered was "not guilty."

The stain upon the young man's name was, therefore, removed, and his father kept his promise, and gave Marie a house. This may have been the cottage at 152 St. Ann Street (now 1020) which was the residence of her numerous family until her death in 1881 at the age of 87. There is no clear record that it was or that it was not.

THE OLD LAVEAU HOUSE.

THE HOUSE IN WHICH MARIE LAVEAU LIVED, 1020 ST. ANN STREET, NEW ORLEANS

The young man, having been set free, went to church frequently to offer thanks for his good fortune. As time went on he brooded over his crime, and associated no longer with his former companions. He became very religious. Finally he sought the girl he had "wronged" and begged her to marry him. She refused. Again he went to Marie and asked her to help him win the girl, for he could not rest until she became his wife and had forgiven him. The Voodoo Queen, now at the height of her glory, told him to have no concern, the girl would marry him within a month. She proceeded to make a concoction of love powder (being ordinary talcum), feathers, pulverized lizard eggs, and the hair of a jackass, which she placed in a bag for him to wear around his waist. She then took strands of hair from various parts of his body and spread them upon the young lady's doorstep.

The girl continued to reject his advances. But one day as he was leaving church he met her just arriving to pray for her aunt who was ill. Upon seeing him she turned suddenly to run away, but stumbled and sprained her ankle. He rushed to her and picked her up gently, begging her to trust him to take her to a doctor and then to her home. She was so impressed by his gentleness and solicitude that she yielded, and the next moment he kissed her. The following day she limped to the altar with him.

New Orleans is rich in folklore. Every old home has its ghosts and many of the superstitions have come down even to this day. Children playing marbles often make strange passes over the heads of companions, jestingly performing strange rites which have not yet been forgotten.

Occasionally, someone will find crossed sticks and a crude circle of salt on their front porch in the morning, pieces of bone stuck in their gate; strange and evil smelling powders sprinkled on their walks and other forms of present day "gris-gris" not a great deal different from those in the days of Marie Laveau.

Voodoo, the dark belief that is supposed to have originated in western Africa, was carried to New Orleans by the first Negroes who were brought to the colony as slaves. Marie Laveau was the most famous of all the queens in New Orleans.

The bamboula was the favorite dance. Its name comes from the fact that the drums used to provide the music for the dance were made from huge joints of bamboo, covered on the ends with skins.

Tales of Marie Are as Strange as the Stories of Noah's Ark

I cannot tell how the truth may be;
I say the tale as it was said to me.

—Sir Walter Scott

The stories concerning the deeds of Marie Laveau are about as controversial as the stories of Noah's Ark or, for that matter, the Ark of the Covenant, Ark of the Revelation, Ark of the Testimony. Noah's Ark was said to be 300 cubits long, 50 cubits broad and 30 cubits high. It was made of "gopher" wood, which has been variously identified with cypress, pine and cedar. This account was for centuries accepted because the dimensions were given by Moses. But in the days of higher learning there were many who questioned the accuracy of this statement; the ship was too scanty for the reception of all the animals and quantity of food required to be stored. To solve this difficulty many of the ancient Fathers and the modern critics almost came to blows—at least some of them lost their religion. Finally an eminent critic computed the size of the ship to be of 81,062 tons, the size of eight of our Liberty ships put together. Here the argument apparently ended. It had lasted about a hundred years, and some grew tired of it. The Ark of the Covenant, Ark of the Revelation, Ark of the Testimony, are the full names of the sacred chest of acacia wood overlaid with gold which the Israelites took with them on their journey into Palestine. Sometimes called the Ark of Yahweh, it was a sacred object of great power, and was carried to every battle. As the ark started it was hailed with the cry, "Arise Yahweh, let thine enemies be scattered, let them that hate thee flee from before thee!" It was an object as much to be feared as Yahweh himself. To presume to fight without it was to invite defeat. As a matter of fact, the Israelites attempted on one notable occasion to attack their enemy without its aid and were defeated. Some have considered that this sacred ark contained some symbol of Yahweh, and it has been held that there were in it some stone fetishes from Yahweh's original abode on Sinai. Others have regarded it as an empty portable throne or receptacle for sacred serpents.

Marie Laveau would have been quite at home in the times of Yahweh, but she did very well in New Orleans. Her snakes were impressive, but snakes are deaf, of course; that is, they have no ears; but they never close their eyes, for they have no eyelids, and it is conceivable that Marie's snakes saw many things unfit for publication, and only repeated in a whisper.

Marie's rituals were, of course, so outrageously vulgar that children were forbidden to witness them, and the adults who attended went secretly, sometimes in disguise, for no person who pretended to be self-respecting could admit that so depraved a performance was enjoyable or even interesting. Marie was the central figure, and she dressed like a gypsy, with a bandana about her head, flashy rings on her fingers and ears, and gold bracelets on her wrists. Her dress was long and full, hanging gracefully from her shoulders. It was always of a dark color. Her eyes, large and brown, sparkled like emeralds against her dark skin. She was the picture of health and vigor. Were she here today in her youth or middle age some motion-picture producer would employ her—for oriental scenery if nothing else.

The ritual, which was held once a week, took place in the yard of her cottage on St. Ann Street, and began with her dancing with the snake (which she called Zombi) wrapped about her. It is said that this snake was 20 feet long and venomous. This is doubtful; it may have been 10 feet, and harmless; nine-tenths of all species of snakes are harmless. When she danced she never moved her feet, only her body, twisting it to the rhythm of the music. But since she was pregnant most of the time during a period of at least 25 years (if she had fifteen children) she probably omitted her dance at infrequent intervals.[3]

After she had led the way, she sat down and gave instructions to her performers. They were men and young girls who danced practically in the nude, usually holding bottles of rum or whiskey from which they drank. Naturally they grew bolder and bolder as the night progressed, and finally indulged in rather intimate love-making in corners of the yard where darkness did not completely conceal them. Meantime the music played louder and louder, and the dancers grew wild; they trembled and shook from excitement; some of them swooned and had to be revived with cold water; others wept and prayed or sang religious songs—they were all hysterical.

---

[3] Before the War Between the States there was a city regulation requiring free women of color to wear bandanas, and after the war this style of head gear became a custom invariably followed, especially by the mammies and household servants.

Many respectable and even prominent men and women of New Orleans attended these orgies. The police often appeared to make a pretense at raiding the place, but they stood in awe of Marie, and after a few words with her went away. After all, there was no law against dancing with a snake, or a fish, which some maintain was another of her dancing companions; there was no regulation against drinking tafia (which was then the drink of the town), nor against praying and singing. The noise was the only basis for complaint, and that was a minor offense. If the revelers drank blood, perhaps from swine, there could be no objection to that; it was good for them; it promoted health. If the police wanted some favor, such as gris gris, or a reading of their fortunes without charge, Marie was ready to accommodate them. They believed that she could bring them luck, and there is nothing a man wants so much as luck, for that seems to be getting something for nothing.

Thus goes the story of Marie's rituals, handed down by the Negro population—generations of it. For years, as far back as the Spanish regime in Louisiana, the Voodoo worship of Africa held interest for a large number of the citizens of New Orleans. The worship was that of the devil, and was first introduced in the city by slavers who found refuge in the dark swamps of the territory. Marie Laveau added scenery, perhaps of a character unknown in Africa. It was dreadful, full of the weird and gruesome, and frightened children away, but greatly impressed the ignorant people of the community. Those of the upper classes who took Marie seriously (and there were many) were more interested in her ability to read minds and foretell events. Apparently they also believed in the power of her gris gris, and her good-luck charms, for they bought them. But it must be remembered that fear is forever in the human mind. There are many proverbial sayings, such as "It is bad luck to pass under a ladder; it is bad luck to put a hat on the bed; it is an indication that bad luck will come if a black cat crosses your path; if you inadvertently put your underclothes on wrong side out it is bad luck to take them off and reverse them; it is bad luck to sew a button on your clothes while you are wearing them." Many people disregard these omens with a laugh, but in doing so consider themselves very brave. (I was once riding with a friend in his auto when a black cat crossed our path. I said, "Look out, a black cat just ran across the road." He said, "you may think that's bad luck, but I know it's superstition, ha ha." He had not gone two blocks when a truck sideswiped his car and tore a fender off—and went on, out of sight.) A cricket on the hearth is good luck; a knife falling on the floor indicates that company is coming (this could be either good or bad luck). There are hundreds of omens, bad and good, which have been accepted, and superstitious people stand in awe of them.[4]

The great Dr. Samuel Johnson, the literary lion of his time and country, would touch every post he passed as he walked the streets of London, and if he missed one he would go back and touch it. That was owing to some fear he harbored in his mind. There is no doubt that he would have been terrifically interested in Marie Laveau. Once when he was told of a terrible hurricane in the West Indies he would not believe it. "It is not true," he said to the person who related the account. "It cannot be true. Don't tell that story again. You cannot think what a poor figure you make of yourself in telling it." Yet he himself related with a grave face how old Mr. Cave of St. John's Gate saw a ghost, and how this ghost was something of a shadowy being. He went himself on a ghost hunt to Cock Lane, and was angry with John Wesley for not following up another scent of the same kind "with proper spirit and perseverance."

---

[4] I recall that on the days I had to walk to school when I was a boy I touched each telephone post as I passed it, and, like Dr. Johnson, if I missed one I would go back and touch it. Once I missed one, and as I was about to go back and touch it a neighbor driving in a surrey stopped and offered me a ride. Thus I missed touching the post, but nothing came of it. I had not yet heard of Dr. Johnson. Unfortunately he was born long before I was, or I could have told him that there was nothing to this business of touching posts.

St. John's Eve

*Awake, my St. John! leave all meaner things
To low ambition and the pride of kings.*

—Pope

The remarkable things that Marie Laveau did are variously mentioned in the guides and other books concerning the history and folklore of New Orleans. Her mind-reading and foretelling events seem to give her a greater claim to fame or notoriety than her Voodoo rituals, which were in character similar to those of the Voodoos of the West Indies.

Her St. John's Eve ceremony, which took place every year on June 23 at a point where Bayou St. John enters Lake Pontchartrain, was a gala affair that attracted the attention of the press, the public and the police. But it is natural to inquire why this blasphemous affair was conducted on St. John's Eve—this mixing of paganism and barbarity with Christianity. Christian hymns, the Lord's Prayer, St. John, and the snake Zombi as a god did not go together. For that matter, nothing seems to have been well planned, for there were the bonfire and the steaming kettles, which seemed out of place in June, one of the hottest months of the summer. The purpose of the "beheaded rooster" which attended the ceremony is not entirely clear. For whatever reason it was there it would have served a better purpose as a meal for some hungry Voodoo. Faustin Wirkus and Taney Dudley in their book, *The White King of La Gonave*, explain the part roosters are supposed to play in such festivals. At a Christmas Eve party in Port au Prince "a priestess darted from the priest's side to where the turkeys and roosters lay, and came back running, a flapping rooster held by the neck in either hand.... She began dancing around the priest with the roosters, dipping, swaying, using them like a Japanese dancer in a circus dancing on a tight-rope with parasols.... She snapped off the neck of the rooster in her right hand so that its body looped through the air and fell twenty feet before her. Before it had struck the ground she dropped its head and changed the other bird from her left hand to her right.... The headless body of the second rooster thumped beside the body of the first, which was still doing a death dance on the trampled courtyard with a score of Negroes in a ring around it trying to keep time with its convulsions."

THE MUSIC GREW LOUDER AND LOUDER
Leslie's Weekly — 1898

There were girls who danced in one-piece garments merely to appear indecent, for if the night was windy there was little of them concealed, or even if the night was calm the breeze which their dancing created left little to the imagination. The men wore loin cloths, the customary dress of the Negroes of Haiti, and, for that matter, South Africa and most tropical countries. In New Orleans when women wore hoop skirts and corsets and men wore stiff shirts and stocks about their necks, the loin cloth seemed indecent—but that is why the dancers wore it. There is an art in showmanship. But there is a deceptive simplicity in art. The grotesque performances of Marie Laveau may not have been entirely agreeable to her, for she is said to have been a very intelligent person, but she had to satisfy her audience. In this she succeeded above all her competitors, and became the central figure in the Voodoo world of New Orleans.

Music filled the air. There was the fiddler with a bottle of tafia beside him, and although he became blissfully and inoffensively drunk he played on through the night. There were also the huge drums made of crude material, all making as much noise as possible, perhaps driving the fish to the middle of the lake and disturbing people who lived miles away. The snake, Zombi, being deaf, was perhaps the only undisturbed creature in the vicinity.

Charms of luck and love-charms were on sale, and nearly every person who attended bought them. The proceeds from this show were sufficient to keep Marie in money for several months. What she did with her money is a mystery, for she lived always in a ramshackle cottage, and never seemed to be affluent. She had many children, but certainly did not send them to colleges, universities or finishing schools; and her husband, if he worked, must have been at least self-supporting. She was, in her way, charitable, and may have enjoyed helping people in need. It is known that she frequently nursed the sick without charge, and even attended yellow fever patients when nobody would go near them. Perhaps she knew, for many things were mysteriously revealed to her, that she was not to contract the fever.

Although nearly everything about Marie's ritual was borrowed from the Voodoos of Haiti, she had to make changes to suit her American audience, and she knew her limits. For instance, a Zombi (i.e. zombie) in Haiti is not a snake, but a soulless human corpse, still dead, but taken from the grave and transformed by the voodoos into a living creature.—"It is a dead body which is made to walk and act and move as if it were alive." This definition is given by W. B. Seabrook in his book, *The Magic Island*. Those who have the ability to create a zombie dig up a body, "galvanize" it into action, and make it a slave, often for the commission of crime, but usually for hard work about the farm. Nobody has ever seen a zombie made, but the Voodoos of Haiti say it is possible, and they show you a zombie—and you dare not contradict them. If you do not believe them they will think you are out of your mind. Man's imagination is a blessing and a curse.

Voodooism in Haiti is a religion, not a circus as Marie made it. But she had a different audience, and, of course, a different purpose; she had to offer a more spectacular show, for even the members of her cult were not as deeply devoted to the Voodoo gods as the Voodoos of Haiti are; and the outsiders who attended her meetings had to be considered in her schemes, for they spent money; they bought her various good-luck charms, and paid for her gris gris, her special services and advice, and her fortune-telling.

Seabrook, in his very interesting book, *The Magic Island*, gives a clear account of a big ceremonial conducted by the priestess of the Voodoos, Maman Célie, who was also a sorceress. He gained her friendship and confidence, and she not only permitted him to attend a ceremony, but divulged to him many of the guarded secrets of the cult. It was a great event, and Celle said to Mr. Seabrook, "all the mountains will be there," and so all the mountains were, for he heard as he traveled toward the meeting place the sound of drums "in the air all around us, everywhere and nowhere, I became conscious of a steady, slow boom... boom... boom... boom. It seemed sometimes to come from a great distance, like rolling far-off thunder beyond hidden valleys and over mountains far away." The "habitation to which we came was a compound, unfenced on a plateau overhanging a gorge, hemmed in by aliveness of their own belief in wonders to be manifested." As the ceremonial got under way he saw the sacrificial beasts—goats, kids, and sheep—dragged into the "tuennelle," and a "mighty chant arose from every throat:"

    Damballa Oueddo,
    Our great Serpent-God.

Presently a woman sang alone:

    It is not today that I will find the path,
    Damballa, I'm ready, but the road is barred.

They seemed to be in great fear that they were not satisfying their "deadly jungle gods" with the "blood of beasts alone." Apparently they thought of human sacrifice; that would have really put them in good standing! Mr. Seabrook was the only white man there. (Had I been in his shoes there would have been running through my mind the thought of how wonderful it would be to sacrifice a white man to bring unending favors from the gods.) What was a sheep or a kid or a goat? They were slaughtered every day for food.

Like Marie Laveau, this priestess Célie had the sorceress-ability to procure for people the things they especially desired. Among her many remarkable deeds mentioned by Seabrook was this:

Her grandson, Paul, had met a young damsel of the mountains who attracted him, but she scorned his advances, and he went to Célie for help. She fabricated a love-charm for him, but it apparently failed of its purpose. When she was informed of this she told Paul to "bring her a humming bird." This was to be a hard task, for humming birds are not plentiful in Haiti. But after some time he procured one; that is, killed one and took it to her. After drying it in the sun she ground it into dust, and mixed with it a few drops of Paul's dried blood and the pollen of some jungle flowers. This dust she placed in a leather bag and gave it to him to wear. On the following day he met the damsel he so much desired, and she passed him laughing, whereupon he threw the dust in her face. With this dust in her eyes and nostrils she became very angry, and swore that she would kill him—"but she lay with him that night in the forest, and on the next morning he fetched her home."

The Queen's Famous Vase and Other Fantastic Claims

There is a paper in the New Orleans Public Library (dated December 1947) by Thomas H. Furlong in which it is stated that no attempt has been made to record the various discrepancies, contradictions, and fantastic traditions which have arisen concerning Marie Laveau. The traditions have, indeed, been recorded, but not the contradictions.

This paper has never been published; it is typewritten, with newspaper clippings attached. There is every indication that Mr. Furlong made a careful research, so far as he went. His manuscript is only seven pages. It is unfortunate that he did not continue his research, for he may have corrected many errors and "contradictions," but he stopped far short of rendering any valuable service in this direction. He apparently accepts as authentic the statement made by Leslie-Leigh Ducros in the Daily Picayune of June 22, 1890, that Louis Philippe gave Marie Laveau a beautiful vase "when he visited New Orleans." According to the story, which is told in newspaper style, Mrs. Walter Saxon painted the old house at 1020 St. Ann Street, which was demolished in 1903, and while painting it the great, great, great, great grand-daughter of the Voodoo Queen showed her this vase, "which was of beautiful workmanship and colors."

"This," she said, "was a gift from Louis Philippe.... I give it to you because you are interested in her and the city she loved. Soon I will be gone—the last of them all—and then it may fall into the hands of the canaille."

"This vase stands now in the unique and historic home of another lover of New Orleans' customs and traditions, Mrs. Helen Pitkin Schertz. And whenever Marie La Veau's name is mentioned, Mrs. Schertz takes it down and shows it and tells the story of how Mrs. Saxon painted the only picture known of the one-time habitat of the Voodoo Queen."

This is all very touching; but why was a "very old" woman in 1890 the great, great, great, great grand-daughter of Marie? and the last of the line? Marie's daughters were all born after 1826 when she formed the liaison with Christophe Duminy Glapion. The oldest was born in 1827, and her child could not have been born until about 1845, and she would have been Marie's first grandchild. Assuming that this grandchild gave birth to a baby eighteen years later, that would have been Marie's first great-grandchild, born in 1863 (about), and she would not have been an old woman in 1890. (There are many persons of middle age living today—1955—whose great-grandparents were born at the beginning of the 19th century.)

Marie Laveau, nearly all writers of her history agree, was born about 1794. Yet this famous vase was given to her by Louis Philippe when he visited New Orleans in 1798. She was then four years old, and about as obscure as any other mulatto girl of the same age. It was not until 1826 that she became prominent as a Voodoo queen.

Captain Christophe Duminy Glapion, according to Furlong, was a man of San Domingo, for he had served at the Battle of New Orleans with the "Company of Men of San Domingo." But his death certificate in the archives of the Civil District Court, New Orleans, shows that he was born in St. John the Baptist parish, and died at the age of 66 on June 26, 1855 in the house on St. Ann Street.

Then it is reported that some member of the Laveau family remarked (before 1903) that seven generations of the Laveaus were born in the house at 1020 St. Ann Street. If this house was given to Marie by a man whose son she helped, after 1826, when she had attained fame, how could seven generations have been born there? A generation (for this purpose) can be computed as about twenty years. Even by crowding time seven generations could not have made their appearance in less than a hundred and forty years.

Much has been written about Marie Laveau, and she has become a figure in the folk-lore of New Orleans rather than a character of its authentic history. Her beauty and her abilities won the people's interest, and often their admiration in her role as the famous queen of the Voodoos. Confucius said, "I have not seen one who loves virtue as he does beauty." The newspapers of her time gave few of the specific incidents wherein she performed wonderful deeds for her clients. Such stories were handed down. The names of the persons who reaped amazing results from her gris gris and mind-reading have naturally been withheld (and no doubt forgotten); yet only they could have testified to the truth of what she claimed. Without any semblance of a date, the stories, perhaps changed many times in the telling, are quite remarkable and extremely interesting.

The newspapers of her time did not seem to favor some of her methods. The Picayune of June 25, 1873, said that she tossed a chicken, feathers and all, alive, into a pot, which, with other ingredients formed a sort of stew, which, if the faithful drank, kept them from the evil eye for a year. "It was hard to believe that in this Christian age, and in this Christian town, there could be such rites practiced unpunished."

TO EAT OF THIS STEW KEPT YOU FROM
THE EVIL EYE FOR A YEAR

MARQUIS DE LAFAYETTE

Did the Marquis de Lafayette Visit Marie Laveau?

Lafayette may have visited Marie Laveau when he stopped at New Orleans for six days during his last trip to the United States. Her grandchildren and other citizens of New Orleans who spoke to people who could remember far back said that he did. But he must have done so after midnight, for every hour of his time here is well recorded by Edward C. Wharton, and published in the Louisiana Historical Quarterly. There is no mention of his visit to the Voodoo Queen. Lafayette arrived at New Orleans on Sunday morning, April 10, 1825. The first day as his carriage halted at the "square" all the bells of the city began to ring, and ten thousand men shouted "WELCOME." The United States troops assembled at the Place d'Armes, and all during the day there were meetings and salutations, speeches, hand-shaking, eating and drinking. There was no time for Marie. On the second day members of the Louisiana Legislature, congressmen, senators from several neighboring states, and thousands of others greeted him and told him what he had done for the United States, and how grateful the people were. On the third day members of the Bar entertained him, and every hour of his time was otherwise taken up until midnight. On the fourth day the Right Reverend William Louis Dubourg, the first Catholic Bishop of Louisiana under American rule, paid him a visit, and there were six other committees waiting for the Bishop to leave so that they could get to him. On the fifth day the "Free men of color," who had served under Jackson (Captain Christophe Duminy Glapion was one of these, but he had not yet met Marie), asked to be received in a body, and Lafayette shook hands with each one of them. Then came the New Orleans Medical Society, and he shook hands with each member. He seems to have had a few hours on this day to relax and do as he pleased and call on the people he wished to see, for he had had enough of the flattering "officials," who were all alike and said the same thing. He drove about the city, but he did not call on Marie—he may have passed her house. He went to see Monsieur and Madame Bernard de Marigny and Madame Catherine Milhet Rousseau, widow of Pierre George Rousseau, formerly a captain in the American Revolution, and Commanding General of the Galleys of the Mississippi, and who had also commanded the brig Galveston under Galvez. That evening he attended a grand Masonic dinner. The next day he left the city.

To list all the engagements of Lafayette would take several pages; the theatre parties, the grand supper, attended by the governor and the mayor, where 800 ladies were seated at numerous tables, all arranged in advance of his coming, and scheduled by the hour. The whole city was lighted up, and all public buildings were decorated. How he attended all the festivities listed is a wonder; he was only 68, but it is remarkable that he survived them. In justice to those who think that Lafayette may have been interested in seeing Marie, it is fair to state that he had been at one time a patient of Franz Anton Mesmer, who introduced into general medicine magnetic therapy based on the laying on of hands; but mesmerism was considered to have some scientific basis, and some of the most eminent persons in Europe claimed that it effected remarkable cures, among them, besides Lafayette, were Marie Antoinette, Schelling, and Schopenhauer. This is as close as we can come to giving Lafayette an interest in Marie—and it is not very close.

Marie Had a Great Interest in the Condemned Prisoners

The Commercial Bulletin of July 3, 1852 published an account of a terrible hanging scene. Under a small heading, "EXECUTION," it stated: "Jean Adam and Antoine Delisle were publicly executed at noon yesterday on Orleans Street, in front of the Parish Prison, for the murder of a negress named Mary in the household of Mr. Chevillon at the corner of Craps and Clouet Streets, in the Third District, in February last. Mary was owned by Mr. Chevillon, and it was in endeavoring to prevent the house from being robbed that she was killed.

"An immense crowd, one of the largest we have ever seen in New Orleans, witnessed the execution, and, as usual on such occasions, much levity was displayed.

"To every right thinking and feeling man who was present, the execution must have been a painful spectacle. At the first attempt to hang the men the ropes broke, and both were precipitated to the ground, a distance of 10 or 12 feet. When brought on the platform again they were bleeding, being wounded, we suppose, by the fall. The ropes were again adjusted; they were again launched from the gallows and the fall being only a few feet, their struggles were shockingly protracted for several minutes.... The seldomer such exhibitions are public the better."

Marie Laveau had somehow got permission to visit prisons at her pleasure on the pretext that her mission was to comfort those awaiting execution and also those who were repenting and expecting to lead a better life when set free. She seems to have taken a fancy to these two criminals, and wanted them to die easily, if they must die. She had served them a good meal on the day of execution. Whether she served wine with this meal is not known, but the two men were intoxicated.

Marie seems to have had a very unusual interest in death, especially in the death of condemned criminals. But she was a great show-woman at heart, and this explains her love of tragedy. Birth and death are the two greatest events in a human life, but there are not nearly so many people at a christening as there are at a hanging or a funeral. Where did we come from and where are we going, that is the eternal question. Had Marie been acquainted with

Shakespeare or the story of the French Revolution she might have satisfied her craving for tragedy in a simple way. But she saw it as it was, in its very making, without the additions or subtractions made by historians.

She was indeed very versatile, and if she had known the history of Genghis Khan she might have turned her attention (more usefully) to infants and predicted for their mothers what they were to become by their birthmarks, if any. He was born in a tent in 1162, and his father, just returning from war at the time, noticed that in his son's clenched fist was a clot of coagulated blood, "like a red stone." This was an omen that he would become a great chief and win many victories. He grew up, unfortunately, and became what his father predicted, a great chief! He massacred 1,600,000 at Herat. "For a whole week the Mongols ceased not to kill, burn and destroy." How could 80,000 men, which was the size of Genghis Khan's army, massacre 1,600,000 persons in a week?—even before the invention of gunpowder, and when the weapons of war were crude and often ineffective? The army was outnumbered twenty to one (taking women and children, of course), and, unless the people stood up and said, "here, kill me, I'm next," which is not likely, for people will fight for their lives, there is some error in the story of 700 years ago, just as there are errors in stories in the time of Marie.

Persons who believe everything they read are at least naïve, for writers have been from the invention of the alphabet the greatest of liars, not that they wanted to be, but they had to be in order to make a living. (Drama is more salable than truth.) In every other respect they are very honest, and in conversation they tell the truth, for that is not to be printed for sale. It is doubtful, for instance, that Herat was a city of 1,600,000, for the population of cities in ancient and medieval times did not run that high. People could not afford to live in cities; they had to camp where they could produce food and kill game—and dodge tax-collectors. It has been computed that during the reign of Augustus (44 B.C.—14 A.D.) the population of Rome was about 1,000,000. The census of 1889 showed, however, a population of 285,625, and it was not guesswork. Rome was, of course, practically destroyed and rebuilt several times. But with no canning plants and deep freeze outfits, city dwellers who liked to eat every day did not fare well; only the soldiers and the aristocracy, who owned everything, and the government workers, who bled the taxpayers, had enough to eat. But this is digressing. This story is about Marie Laveau, whose history is fraught with contradictions and fantastic claims like the history of the ancient chiefs and soothsayers. But in our own times we discover that Washington did not chop down a cherry tree—that was mere fiction to sell his biography; that Lee did not "hand his sword to Grant," and Grant did not say "Lee is my prisoner"—that was mere fiction to sell a book.

A TYPICAL MAMMY OF THE TIME

The Mammy of the Old South Was Not a Voodoo Character

The Mammy of the Old South was a very important servant, the most important in the household, for she was the closest intimate of the family. She was more than a servant; she was a member of the family with unquestioned influence, and in authority she was next to the mother herself, for she dressed the children, put them to bed, got their meals, and advised them concerning their morals and manners. When they grew up they confided in her, for they knew that she was trustworthy so far as they were concerned, and when they married she often became Mammy for their children, and reared them with even greater authority. But this is not to say that any Negro could become a Mammy; she was usually recognized in her youth as a person of good sense, who gave promise of having good judgment, and who possessed qualities of character which suited her for so responsible a position. No person was ever more secure in a position than she was, for she was actually a part of the household, enjoying the glory of the family when it came or suffering its hardships and disappointments. She was a genuine person, sensitive in her way, jealous of "her family," but with no personal ego, and loyal to the death.

There were not many real mammies. The Laveau family certainly did not produce any. It would be at least difficult to trace the family of Charles Laveau or the family of Christophe Glapion very far back, but it is fairly certain that they did not come from the "aristocratic mammy class." They may have been descended from the "blue-bloods" of Virginia or Louisiana or any other Southern state, for during a period of slavery in the United States it was not uncommon for slaveholders to keep slave girls for themselves. In his book, *Black Odyssey*, Rio Ottley states that one prominent planter of Tazewell County, Virginia, kept four Negro girls, for himself and his three sons, and sold their Negro offspring with no apparent feeling whatsoever. He also refers to a strange case in New Orleans wherein E. S. Abdy, who traveled the country from 1833 to 1834, saw a Negro hanged for having illicit relations with his master's daughter. "Her loud avowals that she alone was to blame did not halt the hanging." She died of a broken heart. On the other hand a slave girl had no redress for rape by her master or his sons or anybody of whom he approved. But the master could bring legal action against a rapist—since it involved trespassing upon his property.

Many white men of New Orleans (as well as from all other Southern States) were greatly attracted to the female slave and the free woman of color. The quadroon ball, a fashionable affair in New Orleans, was attended by gentlemen whose designs were to procure concubines, usually among eligible free Negroes (or mulatto) women. This is where Marie Laveau came in for an important part. She operated the Maison Blanche department store for quadroon balls, and from it she derived a good income.

The quadroon balls went out of style long before Marie's death, and what happened to the Maison Blanche is unknown. But Marie had a daughter who attempted to succeed her. Although she was herself very beautiful and possessed personality above the average, she did not have her mother's ability. At least she did not succeed eminently in Voodooism. She was a hit-and-miss mind-reader, and could not rise to perform miracles to dazzle people, and fall to the depths of degradation to disgust them. She did not visit the sick and make them well or nurse them without pay through contagious diseases (as in the case of yellow fever); she did not comfort condemned prisoners. She never did anything really spectacular, and but for her mother's vast reputation her name would never have appeared in print.

To those who embrace Voodooism Marie Laveau and her daughter are saints if not deities, but those who read the lives of saints and the lives of the Laveaus are bound to note a considerable difference between them. The name Laveau is, however, still alive in New Orleans.

As recent as February 19, 1956, a bomb was sent through the mail addressed to Police Headquarters at New Orleans, and exploded prematurely in the post office, doing only slight injury to a clerk. On the previous day Assistant Police Superintendent Guy Banister received a letter containing threats, and signed Marie Laveau III, Queen of the Voo Doos. The letter said: "We are so high you cannot climb over us—so low you cannot get beneath us—and so broad you cannot go around us—so you must go through or by us.... You must go straight and keep your word or else.... You got all kinds of help and now you want to run out on your pledge.... Your name has been handed to us as a rat and double crosser.... To this we give you 10 days warning to get back in line or to where you just left or else stand the consequences. You may run but you can't hide.... We will make you melt away like dry ice in vapor on a hot day and lose everything.... No one will be able to help you."

The Laveaus resembled witches more than they did saints (who ever heard of a saint having operated a house of assignation?), and could be likened to the two witches in the Esquiline Cemetery, the proceedings of which Horace describes. At the new moon they would steal into the cemetery to gather bones and noxious herbs, their feet bare, their hair loose, and their robes tucked up. They alarmed the neighbors with their cries, and making a hollow in the ground would "rend a black lamb over it to summon the dead." Then taking two images, one of wool representing a witch, one of wax representing the man or woman she wished to punish, a magical ceremony was performed: the moon turned red, hell hounds and snakes glided over the place. Then the witches would bury "the muzzle of a wolf and burn the waxed image"; as it melted so faded the life of the prototype. In Greece there were witches so powerful that they were said to be able to make the moon descend from the sky. It is a great wonder that such powers have not been attributed to the Laveaus by the many people of New Orleans who seriously believe that they can still perform miracles.

DANCING ON THE FAIR GROUNDS

THEY ARGUED ABOUT THE SPIRITS
From Gleason's Pictorial Drawing Room Companion — 1854

The Belief in Animism

Marie Laveau did not travel; it is doubtful that she ever left New Orleans in her lifetime or even went as far as Louisiana Avenue (which was then Wiltz Road) on the uptown side of Canal Street. But her fame spread, and the people from the uptown section of the city and even from the parishes along the Mississippi visited her. There were, in fact, many Negroes of the plantations who, having heard of her extraordinary achievements in Voodooism, sought to imitate her. But they were acquainted with Voodooism long before she was born.

These Negroes of the plantations had an abiding belief in animism, and while people of higher culture looked down upon them for that, they should have remembered that their remote ancestors during some period of our civilization worshipped certain inanimate objects and animals to which they attributed a human soul, and they also assigned souls to trees and plants. In classical Europe and the East were Ceres and Demeter, Adonis and Dionysius, and other vegetation gods whose origin can be traced to the corn spirit, which was conceived in some districts in the form of a hare or cock or an ox. In the East Indies wood-choppers endeavored to propitiate the spirit of the tree which they cut down. Briefly, animism is the belief that animals and inanimate objects as well as human beings, have souls, and that their spirits lurk about the earth—the spirits of dogs, cats, horses, human beings, trees, or anything may be encountered.

The plantation Negroes (before Marie's time and after) often found such spirits following them, and they did not dare run, for the spirits could run faster than they, but they trembled and prayed.

Gus Adam, Aunt-Ann, Jack Tinpan and Old Eve Saw Spirits Frequently

There was a Negro, Gus Adam, residing on Olivia plantation in West Baton Rouge parish, who said that a goat with a woman's head followed him from the plantation's gate to his cabin every night if he went home after midnight; but if he went home before midnight, but after nine o'clock, he saw an owl perched on the head of an old woman sitting on a limb of an oak tree which stood in his yard.

He told this to the "preacher" of his church, and he went to see about it, thinking that Gus Adam had probably offended some spirit, and needed to be baptized again. The preacher said that he could talk to the spirits; he knew their language; they talked in Latin, he said, which Gus Adam could not understand. When this preacher arrived, about ten o'clock at night, the spirits of the owl and the old woman were there, and he went close to the tree, muttering something which only he could understand. If the spirits vanished, as he expected they would, that was a good omen, and meant that he had set things right for Gus Adam. But when these spirits remained stationary, and nothing happened, he became angry, and looked about for a rock, found one and flung it up into the tree. As he did so a whirlwind of terrible velocity spun him around, taking his hat high up into the air and tearing off the tail of his coat, leaving only the sleeves and the collar about him. Following this, while Gus Adam was reviving the preacher with a strong drink of corn liquor, a strange light was seen in the sky, and the spirits vanished in a white cloud that came to surround them.

The following Sunday the preacher was to recommend that Gus Adam be excommunicated from the church, for he must have harbored "a grievous crime in his conscience" to bring the wrath of the spirits upon a good preacher who tried to help him. But Gus Adam attended church that Sunday armed with a revolver, for he had got wind of what was going to happen, and he could not stand to be disgraced. When the preacher discovered this he suddenly changed his mind, and said, "It was just a mistake on the part of the spirits, and Gus Adam is as good a man as ever walked in shoe leather." ... But the old woman, Aunt-Ann, who remembered this story, observed that "Gus Adam ain't had no leather shoes on at church that Sunday; he wore canvas shoes he stole from a drummer's samples; but he ain't said nothin'—he let the preacher think they was leather." This she said with considerable chagrin.

Old Aunt-Ann was what might be termed animistic herself, for she frequently complained of a coon that climbed up in a tree opposite her window and fixed his shining eyes upon her; he had eyes as big as saucers, and a tail so long that he wrapped it around the trunk of the tree. There were nights when she couldn't sleep, and when the morning came she was so unstrung that she could not go to her work, which was cooking. When she related this to the owner of the plantation, for whom she cooked, he had the tree cut down and hauled away thinking that would settle matters. But on the following night a goat came and knelt on the stump of the tree, and around it sat six owls with heads bowed as if in prayer. In the course of time old Aunt-Ann hewed out the tree stump and placed nine tallow candles in it which she lit every night. The spirits visited there no more.

Farther down the Mississippi, in St. James parish, lived a woman commonly known as Old Eve. She had never heard of the Laveaus, but with the exception of their ridiculous orgies, she operated very much as they did. Marie Laveau certainly did not bring Voodooism to Louisiana, but it is to her credit that she made it a subject of much publicity. Old Eve worked quietly, and was as good as Marie. Her knowledge of the cult probably came down to her from her African ancestors. The Negroes of St. James parish lived in deadly fear of her, and this gave her incredible power over them. One plantation owner recalls that on a Sunday morning his cook, Linda, arrived for work in great distress and said that when she awoke she found a bag of gris gris under her pillow. This bag contained feathers and human hair. She accused old Eve of having put it there, and vowed that now a curse had been placed upon her she was bound to encounter one calamity after another. In getting the meals that day she burnt the toast to a crisp, cooked the cabbage without salt, and put enough red pepper in the meat to set a whale's mouth on fire. She went about for days frightened by nearly every object she saw, expecting it to "come alive and move on her." Her husband said that he intended to shoot old Eve straight through the head, but just as he said those words rheumatism struck him in the right hand, and he couldn't bend his fingers for several months. Old Eve was powerful.

JACK TINPAN PLAYS A TUNE
TO KEEP THE SPIRITS AWAY

There was a Negro, Jack Tinpan, born on Myrtle Grove plantation in Iberville parish, who actually saw ghosts every night; he saw little men, no taller than a dog, lurking about the yard, carrying tiny lanterns with yellow lights. He was so annoyed by them that he drank a pint of whiskey and went to bed, but they threw stones upon the roof of his cabin, and he was often compelled to get up in the middle of the night and play his banjo, which drove them away; it could not do otherwise, for it also drove the neighbors mad, and some of them threatened to lynch him if he played after ten o'clock at night. He was never lynched, but a Negro who had been kept awake by his playing surprised him one night and broke his banjo into pieces. Since he could not afford another banjo he used a tin-pan to beat the spirits away, and could play a good tune on it, better than he played on the banjo. Obviously, that is where he got the name, Jack Tinpan. His name was Jack, and he had no other name so far as anybody knew.

The Death of Marie Laveau

Marie Laveau died, in her sleep, it is said, on June 16, 1881 at her cottage on St. Ann Street, where she had spent more than half a century. She had, during the last few years of her life, renounced Voodooism and attached herself to the Catholic faith, upon which she had many times in her ignorance brought blasphemy. Her funeral was conducted according to the dignified rites of that church, without a sign of any voodooistic demonstration, and very different from the funerals she had conducted at the prisons and otherwise. She was now a saintly personage. The Daily Picayune lauded her to the sky in an editorial, and made many statements concerning her which were not only incorrect, but ridiculous. It intimated that she was forever smiling (therefore, she was kind), and that her features were "smiling even in death." Persons who knew her did not observe her smiling countenance, but thought of her as a witch, for although she helped friends she also destroyed enemies.

This editorial is, in fact, so full of inaccuracies that it is amusing. It says that Marie Laveau was "born ninety-eight years ago," and when twenty-five she married Jacques Paris. She married Paris August 4, 1819, and it is true that she was at the time twenty-five, for she was born in 1794, but she could not have been ninety-eight when she died in 1881. She was eighty-seven. Her father, Charles Laveau, seems to have been a man of little more than moderate means, for he gave her a house when she was married, but he was not a rich planter, prominent in public affairs, as the editorial states. Then Marie is supposed to have told the reporter who gathered information for the editorial that she recalled a "strange little man with wonderful bright eyes, Aaron Burr, who was so polite and so dangerous." If Burr visited New Orleans in 1806 while attempting to establish an empire to be composed of Mexico, Texas, and Louisiana, it is not likely that Marie came in close contact with him, for she was then twelve years old. He was tried for treason at Richmond, Virginia, in 1807, and being acquitted retired to New York where he spent the remainder of his life practicing law. He lived in comparative obscurity.

Marie spoke of young Governor Claiborne who arrived in 1803 (when she was nine) and his wife and child who died shortly after his arrival, as if she were present. And in the same breath she tells of how the great Frenchman, Lafayette, "kissed her on the forehead at parting." The editorial ends in saying that, "All in all Marie Laveau was a wonderful woman. Doing good for the sake of doing good alone, she obtained no reward, ofttimes meeting with prejudice and loathing; she was nevertheless contented and did not lag in her work. She always had the cause of the people at heart and was with them in everything. During the late rebellion she proved her loyalty to the South at every opportunity and fully dispensed help to those who suffered in defense, of the 'lost cause'.... Her last days were surrounded by sacred pictures and other evidences of religion, and she died with a firm trust in Heaven. While God's sunshine plays around the little tomb (in St. Louis Cemetery) where her remains are buried, by the side of her second husband (Christophe Glapion, to whom she was never married) and her sons and daughters, Marie's name will not be forgotten in New Orleans."

The very last sentence in this editorial is about the only true statement in it. Marie Laveau's name will not be forgotten in New Orleans! It is a wonder that a street has not been named after her. There are many men, among them soldiers, physicians, scientists, and statesmen of Louisiana who rendered a great service to their fellowmen, but even when their names are mentioned there are few who ever heard of them; their deeds, which probably changed the course of history or enlightened mankind and made the span of human life easier and longer, were not as exciting and as dramatic as Marie's were. She knew how to make drama; she never received anyone until her stage was set. It was with her as Du Bartas said in his "Divine Weekes and Workes":

> I take the world to be but as a stage,
> Where net-maskt men do play their personage.

The editor of the Daily Picayune in 1881 was George Nicholson, a very able man, and although his day-to-day movements have not been recorded, so far as we know, it can be assumed that he was on vacation when the editorial on the death of Marie Laveau was written, and if he read that particular issue of his paper when he returned he probably fired the reporter who wrote it. He should have if he didn't, for newspapers are supposed to print facts, and not fiction labeled as facts. There are always two sides to a question, of course, and often three sides, and sometimes as many as four sides (that seems to be the limit), but when a person is trying to build a legend about himself or herself, he or she should not use historical characters to support the story, for they can easily be traced.

MARIE LAVEAU'S TOMB IN ST. LOUIS CEMETERY No. 1
NEW ORLEANS

There are many stories about Marie Laveau which are true, and in themselves remarkable enough to be extremely interesting. For example, there is the story about the very wealthy old man who fell in love with a young girl of moderate means and wanted to marry her. She refused him, but he appealed to her father, who, because of the old man's wealth, was greatly in favor of the match. The girl was in love with a young army officer, and positively refused to give him up.

This gay old fellow, well up in his seventies, was insanely in love, and as a last resort went to Marie Laveau and offered her a good sum of money if she could bring about his marriage to the young lady. She agreed. She first sold him various love-charms, and at regular intervals placed certain characters of gris gris on the doorstep of the young lady's residence. She also kept a candle burning, placing around it certain pieces of the old man's undergarments (which were in those days long and made of the finest wool). Meantime the girl's father, who had lost his fortune and was eager to regain it, continued to do all in his power to persuade his daughter to accept the old man in marriage, advising her that she would before long become a rich widow. But she steadfastly refused, and threatened to kill herself rather than go through with the marriage. "Do not mention his name," she cried, "I never want to see him: I will become a nun; I will never marry." But Marie was working, and every day the old man, suffering the misery of a youthful love, visited her for consolation.

"Do not be impatient," Marie said, "she will marry you."

"How can you say that? How can you say it?"

"I tell you she will marry you," she insisted, "I can't say more than that."

He would then hand her five dollars, sometimes ten, saying, "Here, pray for it to happen; I must have her."

Marie was often impatient with him. "Here, take your money back," she would say, "and pay me when she tells you YES."

"No, keep the money, I trust you."

The old man was sitting in the living room of his palatial residence one morning when a young Negro handed him a note. It was from Mademoiselle, the boy told him.

The old man opened it with trembling hands, and eagerly read its contents. "Very well," he said, as he handed the Negro a five-dollar note, "very well, you can go."

The note merely said: "Monsieur, I have thought it over. Come to see me." This unexpected good news staggered him. It was too much. He felt that he was about to fall, and sat in a chair as he called to his servant to bring him a drink of whiskey. "Make it a full glass—yes, a full glass."

He dressed himself in the afternoon, using his best perfume, and carefully attached to his clothes the love-charm which Marie had sold him. Suddenly it occurred to him that the note was not entirely clear; it may not have meant that she would marry him; it merely said. "I have thought it over. Come to see me." That could be a refusal as well as an acceptance. It could mean anything. This bothered him and he ordered another drink of whiskey, at the same time instructing his servant to order his carriage at once.

When he arrived at the house the young lady rushed to meet him with open arms, and he pressed her close to his bosom (it was unfortunate that he wore a double-breasted vest, a stiff shirt, and a heavy flannel undershirt preventing him from feeling her warmth). She had never been so beautiful. He was speechless.

Finally she spoke. "You received my note?"

"I received it—and it meant — — —"

"Well, of course, it meant — — — yes."

"Those two sentences," he said, "made me the happiest man in the world. You have told your father?"

"Yes, I have told him—and soon the world will know."

The date of the wedding was set that same afternoon, and preparations followed.

The wedding day arrived in due course, and the couple were married. All the prominent people of New Orleans attended, and according to custom there was a dance for which the best musicians had been employed.

The groom, excited and happy, sat conversing with guests who constantly congratulated him upon winning so beautiful a girl. He was old, but he was still handsome, and a gentleman of the first rank.

"Monsieur," somebody cried, "let us see you dance with your beautiful bride!"

He felt tired, and was sorry that this suggestion had been made, but he knew that he must make some pretense of keeping pace with his young bride, not yet twenty. He accepted the challenge, for he knew how to dance; in fact, he danced unusually well. The music started and he was on the floor, apparently as supple as any person there. But before the dance was over his face grew crimson and then purple, and he fell from the arms of his bride. The music stopped. Several men rushed to his assistance. A few minutes later a doctor in the audience pronounced him dead.

His widow inherited his fortune, and later married the young army officer.

Marie asserted that she knew this was going to happen, but she had been entirely sincere in advising the old gentleman that she would arrange the marriage—she had promised nothing more. It is said that she also advised the young lady, who had secretly consulted her, that she would do well to agree to this marriage, for "sooner than she thought" she would marry the army officer. This can be doubted. It is more likely that the young lady had decided to make the best of her bargain, and she honestly intended to be all that is expected of a faithful wife. She probably never consulted Marie. It would have been extremely difficult for her to do so, for a lady of her station had very little freedom; she was watched by a doting mother and guarded by a proud father.

When the Picayune, the Item, and the New Orleans States published laudatory accounts of Marie Laveau the New Orleans Democrat came out (June 18, 1881) with a scathing criticism of her and the papers. The editor was H. J. Hearsay. He said:

> Who has been stuffing our contemporaries in the matter of the defunct Voudou queen, Marie Lavoux? For they have undoubtedly been stuffed, nay crammed, by some huge practical joker. The informant for all is evidently the same, as the stories of the Picayune, Item, and States consist admirably in their uniform departure from historical fact. According to these esteemed but deluded contemporaries, Marie Lavoux was a saint, who had spent a life of self-sacrifice and abnegation in doing good to her fellow mortals, and whose immaculate spirit was all but too pure for this world.... One of them even went so far in his enthusiasm as to publish a touching interview with the sainted woman, in which the reporter boasts of having deposited a chaste kiss on her holy forehead. We are sorry for that reporter if his story is true, for, if he really believes it all, his only consolation is in the fact that greenness is the color of hope. These fictions had one good result, for they created a vast amount of merriment among the old Creole residents, and in fact among all men of mature age who knew the social history of their time in New Orleans.... The fact is that the least said about Marie Lavoux's sainted life, etc., the better. She was, up to an advanced age, the prime mover and soul of the indecent orgies of the ignoble Voudous; and to her influence may be attributed the fall of many a virtuous woman. It is true that she had redeeming

traits. It is a peculiar quality of the old race of Creole Negroes that they are invariably kindhearted and charitable. Marie Lavoux made no exception. But to talk about her morality and kiss her sainted brow—pouah!!!

Marie Laveau's tomb in the St. Louis Cemetery is easily located and easily recognized by the crosses marked upon it, for there are many persons who believe that a wish made while making a cross there will be granted. There are some who take home spoonfuls of earth or twigs from around the grave and carry them home or wear them as good-luck charms. Sometimes these charms bring good results. One man in the habit of betting on horses said that whenever he wore one of them he always won, and had accumulated a fair fortune, but one day when he was betting heavily a pickpocket took it from him with a roll of greenbacks he lifted and he lost every race—went home penniless. It is claimed that a young candidate for the State Legislature made a wish-cross on the tomb, and was elected by a great majority, notwithstanding he was uneducated and unknown in politics, and did not think he had a chance—all he had was the wish, and it "came true."

If the next presidential candidate for the Democratic Party should learn of this wishing-cross affair it might be worth his while to make a trip to New Orleans. There is nothing like faith; it can work wonders. If Joan of Arc had not had faith in the voices she heard from Heaven she would not have raised the siege of Orleans—but it is a great pity that she did, for she was sentenced to be burned at the stake as a result, to the shame of all concerned in the matter, the Burgundians who betrayed her; the English who wreaked their revenge against her; Charles VII whose throne she saved, and who made no attempt to save her; the Catholic Church, and the people of France. She has been in late years canonized by the Catholic Church, which granted her a second trial about five hundred years after her death, and pronounced her innocent and a person of great merit. She would have been no doubt just as well satisfied to have her young life spared and to have been forgotten after she died a natural death.

To all the educated Negroes and white people of New Orleans Marie Laveau is dead, and her strange history is of considerable interest; but to the ignorant and superstitious her spirit is still lurking about the city, and frequently appears to do good or make trouble, for to some she is a saint, to others she is evil.

There Were Other Strange Characters

There was a mulattress, Fanny Mosebury, who lived in New Orleans some years ago, and while she was herself quite remarkable for her psychical powers she was forever encountering spirits; they came to her room and often turned her bed upside-down or took feathers out of her mattress, and tramped on her roof, stopped her chimney and caused her room to fill with smoke. One night there was a man sitting on her doorstep; she knew him slightly, and told him to move, for there was a spirit (supposedly Marie Laveau) that did not like him, and would certainly give him trouble. He had left his wife when she became pregnant and "taken up" with another woman. He scorned her warning with the remark, "I ain't scared of no spirit doing nothin' to me, ha, ha!" Whereupon he complacently lit a cigar, and began to puff clouds of smoke into the air, and Fanny closed the door on him. But suddenly a chill came over him, and the light of his cigar went out. His hands began to tremble, and when he attempted to rise (intending to run away from the scene) he found himself in the position of one glued to his seat, and his knees would not bend or unbend—or if they did he was too weak to move.

Then something like a heavy hand pushed his hat over his eyes and slapped his face.... As he attempted to call Fanny a hand was pressed over his mouth, and a voice said, "Go and pray and respect." Presently he felt his strength returning, and was soon able to lift the hat from his eyes, and as he did so he saw a very beautiful mulatto girl standing near him, the image of Marie Laveau. She vanished as suddenly as she appeared. He then staggered up Fanny's steps, and she admitted him into her room, which was gloomy, with pictures of saints pinned up on the walls, red lamps burning, and images on every table and on her dresser. When he related what had happened she gave him a crucifix to wear, and told him to go back to his wife, never to leave her. To this he would not agree, for his wife had once threatened him with a knife, he said, and he never wanted to see her again.

Fanny took a deck of cards from a drawer of her dresser and cut it four times. "I see that fight," she said, "and it was the night you beat her; I see blood, and a torn dress, and I see a child crying, and a pistol on a table right by a Bible. But I don't see no knife."

"She had it hidden in her dress," said the man, "she sho' had."

Fanny cut the deck again and spread the cards upon the table. She was hardly satisfied with what she saw, and she cut the deck another time. "They show," she said, "that she ain't had a knife, but told you she had, and she'd cut your hand if you reached for the gun. You had already hit her and made her nose bleed."

This was pure mind-reading. She had described the fight exactly as it occurred.

The Negro began to tremble again. "How'd those cards tell you all that? Lord, have mercy; that's just how it was. I feel something coming on me; I can't stop trembling; oh, Lord, Miss Fanny, give me a drink of whiskey, please!"

Fanny had no whiskey, but gave him a dose of aromatic spirits of ammonia, which she kept in the house for her frequent use.

He was revived, and the trembling stopped. "I see the way," he said, "and I'm going—I'm going back to Martha, Lord help me."

According to the account, he did go back to his wife, and later, having prepared himself with the study of theology and philosophy became a preacher of no mean ability. (What this Negro's real name was I never knew, but I think he called himself Brother Howard. I went to his church many times, and heard excellent preaching, good singing, extremely good music, and saw worthwhile scenery. The throne was decorated in red, gold, and silver, and the preacher wore a white and scarlet robe. The "sisters" who played and sang wore uniforms of white and blue. They were all supposed to be blessed with psychical powers, and at intervals they went through the congregation soliciting questions from those who were in trouble, and offering to help by prayer and otherwise. I recall one man in the congregation saying, "My name is Ted Jones; my wife has kidney trouble, and is very sick." The sister advised, "give her a pitcher of lemon juice and water tonight, and we'll pray." The preacher repeated, "we'll pray!" Then the sister said, "fear not; she'll be well tomorrow." To make certain that Mrs. Jones would recover the preacher lit a candle, and kneeling beside it said a solemn prayer. It was reported at the church during the next meeting that Mrs. Jones had recovered).

Fanny Mosebury can be referred to as a saintly woman. She was for many years employed as a cook in a very aristocratic family of New Orleans, whose wealth and influence finally dwindled away, but she never deserted them; when they could not pay her the wages to which she had been accustomed she accepted less and less, and finally offered to work for no wages at all. She nursed them when they were ill, and regardless of the hours she worked would accept no pay. She also reared her children and many of her grandchildren. Yet she was so impoverished that often the only heat she had in winter was from old newspapers she could collect to burn in her grate. Finally some people who knew her and those for whom she had worked so faithfully appealed to the Division of Public Welfare and arranged for her to receive a small income from that source until she died about fifteen years ago.

HE CALLED FOR HELP; THE SPIRITS WERE AFTER HIM

Outwitting the Yankee

Gus Adam was a very fine old Negro who worked hard for a living, being a woodchopper on John Martinson's plantation. He attended church every Sunday, and brought his children up in "fear of the Lord." He had only one fault, he'd steal anything he could lay his hands on. He was otherwise so good and kind-hearted, especially where children and animals were concerned, that even when Mr. Martinson discovered his thefts he did not have the heart to prosecute him. Sometimes he even refrained from accusing him, or when he did he accepted his explanation that he "merely took that thing by mistake; and would put it back or pay for it."

But Mr. Martinson, being in every way all too generous for his own good, lost his plantation to his creditors, who placed in charge of it a Mr. Ambrose Silent from New York, a very avaricious and unfriendly man.

Mr. Silent had been in the great plantation mansion only a few weeks when he missed his watch, which was very valuable. This upset him to so great an extent that he called the sheriff and asked him to search all the houses in the Negro quarters for he had been told that all Negroes were thieves, which was, of course, untrue. He went with the sheriff to do the job, and when they came to Gus Adam's house, Mr. Silent said, "there's no use searching the woodchopper's house, for he never comes near the mansion, and, moreover, he is a fine character; that I discovered a few days after I arrived."

"How so?" asked the sheriff.

"As I was riding in the woods where he was chopping logs my horse stumbled and sprained his ankle. This man took off his shirt, belt and suspenders, and with them made a bandage for my horse, enabling him to limp home."

"That's very commendable," said the sheriff, "but you will find your watch in his house."

"Do you know him?"

"Oh, yes, very well."

"Is he a habitual thief?"

"That's his reputation."

"Has he ever been to jail?"

"Not that I know of."

"How long have you been sheriff?"

"Thirty years."

"And you've never put this thief in jail? Frankly, I do not understand that. You must be lax in your duties; but I'm here to tell you that I'll not stand for stealing, and this man must go to jail."

At this moment Gus Adam was seen coming down the headland of the field with his axe on his shoulder. Mr. Silent and the sheriff waited for him.

"Lord hev mussy," said he as he approached and looked inquiringly at the two men, "if it ain't de sheriff. How'd-do sheriff—and Mr. Silent. Is you lookin fo' somethin'?"

"Yes," said Mr. Silent, "we're looking for my watch."

"You mean that fine gold watch that's got a silver band 'round it?"

"That's it," said Mr. Silent.

"You ain't done lost dat watch, Mr. Silent? But yo' sho' is or you'd not be lookin' fo' it."

The sheriff was nettled by Adam's complacency. "Never mind beatin' around the bush. Where's that watch?"

"Sah, I was just about to tell you, but if you'se 'cusing me when you ain't got no reason in de world, I'll just throw up my hands and say, Lawd, let 'em take me to jail if human beings is lak dat."

"That's just what I'll do," said the sheriff as he took a pair of handcuffs from his pocket.

"Just a moment there," said Mr. Silent, "I don't know how you people do business down South, but you can't put a man in jail on mere suspicion."

The sheriff's authority had never been questioned before, and this made him very angry. "I think we know our business pretty well, Mr. Silent, and I'm taking this man to jail."

"No, you're not," said Mr. Silent calmly, but forcefully. "I prefer to handle the matter myself."

The sheriff took this as an unpardonable insult. "I'll bring a charge against you for harboring a criminal," he cried.

"Do as you like," said Mr. Silent.

The sheriff then went on ranting about what he was going to do. "This is a government of law, not of men. Please remember that, Mr. Silent."

"Yes, I've seen that on your courthouse, but in my opinion it's so much bunk."

"Why, you damn Yankee," shouted the sheriff, "insulting our laws, insulting our courthouse, and an officer of the law. I'll see to it, I'll see to that, I assure you." With this he put the handcuffs back into his pocket and started off, still talking. "Why, think of insulting a Southern gentleman who has the honor to be sheriff, and protecting a damned thief, a known thief." By the time he reached his horse Mr. Silent could no longer distinguish what he was saying, but he did not think it was anything complimentary.

When the sheriff had gone Gus Adam came to life. He had pretended to be in a dejected state, as if he had lost interest in life and cared not what happened. "Mr. Silent," he said, "you is a fair gentleman."

"Thank you. But let me have my watch."

"I knows yo knows that I ain't got dat watch, Mr. Silent, or you'd o' let de sheriff take me. You ain't lost dat watch; I seen you put it in the pocket o' your saddle."

This confused Mr. Silent. He could not recall a pocket on his saddle. At least he had never used it. "There's no pocket on my saddle, Gus Adam," he said.

"Thar sho' is, Mr. Silent. Mr. Martinson done kept money in it all de time. It's sho' thar."

"I didn't put my watch in it."

"You did, sah, and I seen you did it, and I hope de Lawd may strike me daid if I didn't."

"When did you see me put it there?"

"Was the night 'fore last, in de middle o' de night, I saw you put it thar."

"This is utterly insane, Gus Adam. Are you in your right mind?"

"I sho' is."

"I was asleep. I went to bed at ten."

"You sho' did, but you got up."

"What are you trying to do, make a fool of me?"

"I sho' ain't, Mr. Silent; I'm tellin' you God's truth."

This was too much for Mr. Silent to take in. He did not understand the Southern Negro; he did not know how naïvely clever and crafty he was. "Let us go and see if the watch is where you say it is."

He and Gus Adam walked toward the horse, which was hitched to a post not far away.

"You'll sho' find it thar, Mr. Silent."

"I doubt it. I begin to doubt everything," said Mr. Silent as he examined the saddle. "I see no pocket."

"Thar it is." Gus Adam pointed to a pocket in the rear of the saddle.

Having discovered the pocket, Mr. Silent searched for the watch, but found nothing. "There's no watch here."

"Must be. Lem-me see," said Gus Adam as he ran his hand into the pocket and pulled out the watch. "Sho' is."

"Well, it wasn't there when I reached for it."

"Sho' was, Mr. Silent. That's a double pocket."

Then Mr. Silent ran his hand into the pocket again and found that it had two compartments. "Now," he said, "explain to me how that watch got there. I don't believe what you said about my putting it there."

Gus Adam put half a pack of Red Cross tobacco into his mouth and proceeded to explain. "You see, de mansion you live in is haunted since Mr. Martinson left, and on this place, unbeknown to you, is a witch what has supernatural power. She can make people git up in their sleep and walk about and do damage, and they never knows what they've done. She's in wid de spirits o' Mr. John's ancestors who owned this place about the time of King Charles, a Spanish gentleman, and they tells her what to do. She made you git up and hide dat watch in dat place, de pocket o' yo' saddle. I was a-comin' down de road, and she said if I told she'd put a curse on me, and I couldn't work no mo', nor chop wood. And my legs is gettin' stiff now. But I figured I'd better get the curse than go to jail."

"You expect me to believe that?"

"I sho' don't. But it's true."

"Where is the witch?"

"That I sho' can't tell. No matter what you do to me, she'll do worse."

"Then it stands like that. But in the third house down the row there is a woman that looks like a witch. Let's go there. I'll do the talking."

"I kaint move, Mr. Silent."

"You don't mean that. You're faking."

Gus Adam was not "faking." He could not move. "She told me not to tell." he moaned, "she sho' did, she sho' did."

A strange feeling came over Mr. Silent. He looked up in the sky and saw a dark cloud shaped like a warship. He wondered what was happening to him. It was now late in the evening, and the warship, floating against the setting sun, seemed to be illuminated inside. He had never seen anything like it before. And there stood Gus Adam unable to move because a curse had been placed upon him. This also was a new experience to him. "Where is the witch?" he cried in desperation. "I'll have her put off the place. Tell me, Gus Adam."

"Don't git no curse on you lak I hev. Please don't, Mr. Silent."

"Nobody can put a curse on me."

GUS ADAM, AN HONEST THIEF

"Dey sho' kin. Be mighty careful."

The cloud, still shaped like a battleship, floated on, faster now, and its lights grew dim, for the sun was on the horizon; there were traces of men and cannon aboard, and a grayish smoke seemed to be pouring out of the smokestacks. The hands of the plantation were coming from the field; they seemed tired and lifeless, as if they were all Zombis. And there stood Gus Adam unable to move. "Just look at dat warship," he said, "it ain't no good sign." Mr. Silent felt alone and lonely; he wished himself back in New York.

Presently he beckoned to two Negroes on their way homeward. They stopped.

"What's your name?" he asked one.

"Joe Brown."

"What's your name?" he asked the other.

"John Washington."

"Then you two men pick up Gus Adam and carry him home. He can't walk."

The two men, both as strong as mules, lifted Gus Adam with ease and conveyed him straight to his bed. His wife proceeded to rub him with a compound of hot mustard and red pepper, a preparation of her own which was never known to cure or kill, but she said it was a good remedy, for it took your mind off of what "ailed you and put it on the burning skin, which was nothing serious."

"What's de trouble?" asked John Washington.

"De witch."

"Oh, de witch. She's terrible."

"I'll go see her," said Joe Brown. "She ain't got no business puttin' de curse on no workin' man lak you."

Although Mr. Silent went home determined to forget the matter, and to write home about it in a humorous vein, he slept fitfully that night. The battleship in the sky, the curse on Gus Adam, and the witch occupied his thoughts. All during the night he heard noises, as if the walls of the great house were cracking, and there were times when he thought he heard shrieks. But he was a sensible man, and brave, not in the least superstitious. He would laugh it off. He was anxious to write the letter—to his mother; he was not yet married, although he was well over forty.

The light of the morning was very welcome to him, and he opened his window to watch the rising sun as its rays played upon the green leaves and the blossoms which were just appearing, for it was early spring. He dressed leisurely and went downstairs to advise his cook, a stout Negro woman whose name was Cinderella, that he was ready for breakfast. But as he reached the great hall he was amazed to see blood tracks, the shape of a human foot, leading to the kitchen. He called for Cinderella, but there was no answer. He hurried to the kitchen; it was empty and dismal.

His first thought was of Gus Adam, and he went straight to his house, expecting to find him in bed and helpless. He tapped the door lightly as one would do in the case of the sick.

A woman opened the door. "You lookin' fo' Gus, Mr. Silent? I'm his wife. Yassa. My name's Bee. But he's gone—out choppin' wood."

"Then maybe you can help me."

"I'll sho' try."

"Then tell me this: where is the witch? Where is Cinderella? What's this all about? Am I—have I been dreaming or has this actually happened?"

"I sho' don't know what you talking about, Mister."

"Don't tell me you don't know what I'm talking about. You saw your husband carried into the house. And then I woke up this morning and found blood stains on the floor of my hall. And Cinderella didn't come to work. Where is she?"

"Sheriff come got her last night."

"What are you talking about?"

"Just what I says. The sheriff come got her."

"What for?"

"You ain't heard about de cuttin' scrape?"

"I thought I heard shrieks, but I thought it was my imagination. I was half asleep."

"Sho' was terrible. Joe Brown and John Washington, dey went to get Cinderella to take the curse off Gus, and she said she ain't goin' do nothin', but would put mo' curse on him; den de fight started, because Cinderella's husband come out and meddled. She stabbed John Washington bad, and he cut her on de foot. She run in your house to hide when Joe Brown's boy got on his fast horse to call de sheriff. He lives right on de next place."

"Just a minute," said Mr. Silent, as he motioned to her to stop talking so that he could ask a question. "Is Cinderella the witch? Do you mean to tell me that? "

"I sho' didn't mean to tell you, fo' I ain't supposed to know."

"Then," said Mr. Silent, "the witch was my cook! If that doesn't beat everything. That's the last straw."

There was something in this tale that didn't seem clear to Mr. Silent. Why was Gus Adam out cutting wood if Cinderella had refused to take the curse off him? He asked Bee.

She had a ready answer. "When Joe's boy went for the sheriff she done took de curse off Gus—so she can appear innocent. That's all. He tuck 'er to jail anyway. But she'll be out 'fo night. De sheriff ain't gon' fool wid her; he sho' ain't. She already done put gris gris in his pocket, dey tells me; Sam Huston's wife done pass here and told me that, and she say his horse's just running up and down de yard, lik wild."

"Well," said Mr. Silent as he walked away, "you people are too smart for me—too smart, entirely too smart."

The Burley Landing Election

There was a man in the village of Burley Landing known as a half-wit, and although he had a very fair command of English and could out-talk a preacher or a lawyer (or it was said he could) nobody took him seriously. The townspeople enjoyed playing practical jokes on him. His name became a synonym for "foolishness." A mother correcting her child would say, "you act like Becknel Lekay." That was his name. His father had been a saloon keeper, and that gave him some social prominence, but he could not hold a job of any kind, and, therefore, never worked.

There was to be an election for mayor in Burley Landing, an office which paid six hundred dollars a year, and the citizens, being dissatisfied with the conduct of the present mayor, Nom Bly, who spent his time in the coffee house under the influence of liquor, decided that they would find two candidates to run against him.

A committee composed of the leading men of the village met to select the opposing candidates. Nobody seemed very interested in the office. But under pressure a Mr. Henry DeLux agreed to become a candidate, and said that he would, of course, "walk away with the election" ... "But who will be the other candidate?" somebody asked. "Let us pick somebody who ain't got no chance—merely to split the ticket."

"How about Becknel Lekay?"

Everybody laughed. "That's a good idea. Run him as a joke."

"Indeed!" came a voice, "he'll be the joker in our deck."

When Becknel Lekay was informed that he had been selected as a candidate he was elated. "That reminds me of the honor conferred upon George Washington," he exclaimed, "and I shall serve my country with the same zeal and honesty."

This statement brought much laughter, and was repeated all over the village in a few hours.

There lived on a plantation adjoining the village an old Negro woman who practiced sorcery and told fortunes. She was called the River-witch, and nobody knew her by any other name. This title was given her years before, derived from her custom of sitting on the bank of the Mississippi to communicate with the waves and the current, which, she said, "brought, her messages, and told her wha' de world had been and wha' it was gwine, and wuh it had to say fo' itself." Anytime anything happened she said, "I knowed it, de waves done told me so."

After Becknel had made his famous speech upon becoming a candidate, he went to this River-witch for help and advice. He found her cooking popcorn and boiling syrup to make popcorn balls, which she sold on the plantation.

YOU CAN'T DISCUSS POLITICS CALMLY

"River-witch," he said, "I'm a candidate for mayor of Burley Landing, and am aiming to win. My name will go down in history like George Washington and Abraham Lincoln. My picture will be in the school books."

"Lem-me git dis popcorn made 'fo I tak you' case, Mr. Lekay."

"I will show the people how a government should be run," Becknel Lekay continued, "and, I will close everything on Sunday, even the churches that's staying open too long and tiring the people out. Sunday is a day of rest, the Lord said. I'll put the street lights out at midnight, and let the ghosts scare the revelers home."

The River-witch went on making her popcorn.

Becknel Lekay continued, "The rich will pay the taxes, the poor will pay nothing. There will be better streets and better sidewalks. Taxes will be higher, but the town will be a show place and people will come from miles around to see it—from as far as New Orleans. I will build a new courthouse, and a new city hall, taxing the rich and sparing the poor. I will change the name of Burley Landing to Burley City, and the parish in which we live will become known as Lekay parish."

The River-witch finished her popcorn balls, and threw them into a pan. "Yo' sho' gwine git elected," she said.

"I'm glad to hear you say that, for my hopes are high."

"Dese ha' pop-cones ain't gwine sell 'til Sat'day when de Negroes gits paid off, so we's gwine to de river to see what de current say."

She then put a rabbit's foot in a small bag, and gave Becknel the skull of a cat. "You gwine git sounds thru dat."

Having locked her door securely and having also padlocked her front gate, she started toward the river with Becknel. The current was swift, for it was late in April and the river was rising. Logs in great numbers were floating southward. The River-witch and Becknel sat on an old up-turned skiff which had floated ashore.

"Now put dat skull to yo' ear, and you gwine huh talkin'."

Becknel obeyed, but only the sound of the waves splashing on the shore came to him. "I hear nothing, River-witch."

"Den, gim-me dat skull, I gwine tel' you wuh's comin'." She held the skull close to her ear. "Yo' mus' be deef if yo' ain't heaud nothin'—if you' ain't heaud dem voices. Dey say: You's a plum fool if yo' think yo' gwine git 'lected on any such talk as yo' spoutin' out dat's in yo' mind. Dey say yo' ain't to do no talkin' bout taxes, but promise all de fine buildin's an' schools and easy livin' as if dey was to com' out o' yo' own pocket. Don't tell nobody wha' yo' gwine git de money—just promise."

"Does that come from the current, actually as you are telling me?"

"Sho. It sho' comes plain. Dere's a great spirit talkin, it must be George Washington hisself. He say, tell dem people de Lawd done tell yo' how to make every man rich and git every woman a husband, an' every man a wife, and dat you'se gwine sho' de ole people how to git young an' de young people how to stay young. Dat's all yo' got to do, and you'll git elected."

"River-witch, that's all I wanted to know. When I'm mayor you'll never have to work. You'll be the scrub-woman in the new City hall."

THE RIVER-WITCH — SHE GETS MESSAGES
FROM THE CURRENT

This revelation of the current and the waves satisfied Becknel, and he and the River-witch left the river bank. He went home and wrote up his speech which was in substance what the spirits of the current and the waves told him to say.

The people went to hear him, crowds of them, and they laughed at what he said. The single men said, "Becknel is going to get us a wife," and they laughed. The old maids said, "Becknel is going to get us a husband," and they laughed. The old men said, "Becknel is going to show us how to get young when he is mayor," and they laughed. The young people said, "Becknel is going to show us how to stay young, but we don't care for that," and they laughed.

Just before the time for voting Mr. DeLux made a grand speech. He said that the people had had a good time listening to Becknel Lekay, but now he had come to talk seriously, and urged them to elect him because he was a sober business man, and would not spend his time drinking in the coffee house like the present mayor; that he intended to put the village on a business basis, see that taxes were collected and that improvements were made. He said that Nom Bly had not bestirred himself to solicit votes, for he could not take the time from the coffee house, and yet he had made the remark that the election "was in the bag"; he didn't have to worry the people with such clownish orations as Becknel was carrying on and as Mr. DeLux was preparing. "Well, we'll see," said Mr. DeLux, "I'm your next mayor." He smiled. "We all know, of course, that Becknel is a joke. If he could carry out a tenth of his promises I'd vote for him myself."

When election day came Nom Bly was at home recovering from delirium tremens, but still seeing snakes, lizards and black cats which crawled about his bed. Two doctors, both his supporters, attended him, but could not persuade him that the snakes, lizards and cats were not menacing him.

Mr. DeLux spent the day announcing to the people why Nom Bly was not about on a day so important to him. "The man has delirium tremens. Elect him, and that's what you'll get for a mayor."

Becknel Lekay went about crying, "Believe what I tell you; it came to me from the High Heavens, and remember the moon is in the sky, and it moves the ocean, makes the tides rise, makes plants grow, and the secret of all this I have. There are wonders in the world that you have never heard of."

When the time came for counting the votes the most conspicuous man there was the saloon keeper who owned the coffee house in which Nom Bly spent his time. His name was Jack Kembul.

"I want to see the votes counted," he said, "and don't want any funny business just because Nom Bly is sick."

"They'll be counted right," said Mr. Henry DeLux, "but you ain't got a right here."

"No? Maybe not. But I've got something in my pocket that'll purty nigh give me the right."

"The moon is in the sky," said Becknel, "and the man within it watches you, and he controls the tides of the sea."

"Are you drunk? or just a plain fool?"

"Never had a drink in my life."

"No, you don't need to!"

"The pen is mightier than the sword," cried Becknel, "and I have writ my speech."

"And you ain't drunk!" said the saloon keeper. "I wouldn't be surprised if you got one or two votes at that."

The commissioners counted the votes as the saloon keeper stood over them with a gun.

When they had finished counting and arrived at the totals Becknel inquired who had won.

"We don't know yet, Becknel, but you've lost. You ain't in the running and that's all we can say."

"Then to me it's doom and death," said Becknel, "for no man can stand so great a disappointment. I'll only stay until you find out who won."

The saloon keeper made a motion with his gun as if he meant business. "Let me see them tally sheets."

"Hey, not so fast there," said the commissioner, "it seems that the tie is between Henry and Nom."

"Let me see them sheets," the saloon keeper demanded again. "Lay them on the table."

The commissioners obeyed, and the saloon keeper inspected the sheets carefully.

"Why, you dam thieves, there ain't no tie a' tall. Becknel Lekay has won more than three to one. You can't make no crooked deal with me." He turned to Becknel. "You're elected mayor!"

Becknel fainted, but was quickly revived with a cold towel, and when he came to he said, "I accept the responsibility, and the man in the moon will guide me."

The town's weekly came out on the following day with Becknel Lekay's picture on the front page and said he would make the best mayor Burley Landing ever had, for he was a man of vision.

In the course of a year Becknel Lekay had become a very wealthy man. He had not kept a single promise he made to the people, had not even kept the promise he made to the River-witch, who continued to sell popcorn balls for a living. The man in the moon had forsaken him, and the devil had got hold of him. That was the talk that went around. Nom Bly had been a drunkard, that was granted, but he was honest, and did not take graft. He was still a poor man after thirty years in the "mayor's chair," or, more properly speaking, in a chair at the coffee house.

Becknel Lekay had become very pompous. He received only men of recognized influence; to others who called "the mayor was too busy." He floated in the best society, and had persuaded a New Orleans girl to marry him. She led him a swift life, and supported her father, mother, and two sisters on his money. They had all quit working. But that pleased him, for it gave him prestige, and his in-laws fed him flattery, which made him very happy. He employed an able artist to make two paintings of him; one he hung in the city hall, the other in the village high school. His picture was not yet in the school books, but that would come years after his death, he said.

The reader is naturally wondering how Becknel Lekay became very wealthy from graft in a comparatively small village. Here is the explanation: A month or two after he took office three night clubs opened up in the town and people from neighboring cities (where gambling was prohibited) flocked to them. There were in addition horse-racing, dog fights, cock fights, and various games. Burley Landing had become a gambling resort.

Although Becknel prospered he made enemies as well as friends, and among his enemies was the River-witch. She spent nearly every night on the bank of the river, listening to the current and the waves. One evening she saw a nicely dressed young lady walking on the levee and leading a little dog by a leash. She hailed her. "Hey, you. Lady, dat levee's mighty steep, but I's gwine to git up dare an' talk to yo'."

This lady was Mrs. Becknel Lekay.

"Well, I'll wait. But hurry, for I'm walking my dog, and am just about to turn around."

"Yessum. You'se sho' gwine turn 'round," said the River-witch as she slowly made her way up the levee. And she was thinking that if this young woman were "the right sort" she would have come down to an old woman. "Yo' sho' act lak a queen," she said as she reached the top of the levee.

"I don't know whether that's a compliment or a piece of impudence," said Mrs. Lekay.

"Yo' ain't know me?"

"No, I don't. If you're looking for a job, I've got all the servants I need. If you want money, I have no change."

The River-witch thought of the day she sat on the river bank with Becknel Lekay and gave him "the words of the spirits that made him mayor." She took a rabbit's foot and the skull of a cat from her bag. "You ain't seen nothin' lak dis, is you?"

Mrs. Lekay was frightened. "What are you trying to do, scare me? I'll have you arrested, and quick, for my husband's the mayor."

"Dat I sho' do know. But I'm de River-witch."

"The River-witch? What do you mean?"

"Yo' ain't never heard o' me, but de mayor is. Yo' can tell de mayor dat de current and de waves done tole de River-witch dat he's gwine to jail."

"Why, you impudent old thing," cried Mrs. Lekay, "I'll see that the sheriff picks you up before dark." With this she turned and hurried back to the village.

When she told her husband what the River-witch said he was greatly upset. "Why did you walk on the levee? Why did you talk to her? She's an evil woman; she can put a curse on you and that's what she's done. I think I'll go and jump in the river. Don't come near me; the curse is on you, but I'll catch it. Why weren't you polite to her?" He raved on as his wife stood amazed. "I was a good man until I met you. Get out of my house. Pack and go."

"Are you crazy? You are, you are, you are a lunatic. That old woman—what is she to you? What is she to anybody? Tell me."

Becknel Lekay armed himself with a revolver and walked out of the house. "I'll see," he said as he went through the door, "I'll see who can command the man in the moon."

He went to the house where the River-witch lived, but she was not there. He searched the river bank, but did not find her. He searched nearly all night, but with no success.

Finally he went home, and slept fitfully for a few hours. But when he awoke the sheriff delivered him a notice to appear before the grand jury on the following day.

He was indicted for graft, tried fairly, and sentenced to a term in jail. Since he was removed as mayor the citizens of the village acting through a committee, agreed to give old Nom Bly another chance, and on his promise that he would drink only after sundown he was appointed mayor.

Becknel Lekay's in-laws went back to work, and the River-witch continued to sell her popcorn balls on the plantation.

The paintings of the former mayor are still hanging in the city hall and in the village high school. They are faded and dusty, but nobody inquires who the man is or why his picture hangs on the walls.

Charles the Grinder

There was a Negro in West Baton Rouge parish called Charles the Grinder who went about the plantations and villages offering to sharpen scissors, knives, plows, tools or anything that needed sharpening. He never worked more than half a day, for he said "a man who works half time lives twice time, and in relaxation there is double expectation, scientifically speaking." Translated this meant that a lazy man lives twice as long as a hard-working and ambitious man. He never worked for wages, his reason being that the hours were too long, and pay-days too far apart. But he made ten times as much money as any laborer ever made in those days (about 1905), for he was a Voodoo priest (so he said) quietly practicing his profession, and bleeding the Negroes white. His sharpening business was merely a blind, but he made money from that, too, for he was an expert at it; he could sharpen a common pocketknife to split a hair.

He had been a seaman, and remained for some years in Haiti, where he became acquainted with Voodooism, and said that he taught the Voodoos in New Orleans (including Marie Laveau II—which, of course, was not true), and was "run out of the city because of my superior knowledge." He lived in a houseboat on the Mississippi, and it was there he conducted his Voodoo rites, secretly and for his own purpose. He kept a snake in a box; and a rooster with golden feathers, tame as a cat and fat as a pig, strolled about his boat, sometimes flapping its wings and spreading gold dust on the floor. Charles said the dust was pure gold, and the rooster was a "golden legend." What he meant by that nobody ever knew. He loved to use big words, and whether they were in the right place of a sentence to make sense was of no importance to him. He kept a large stock of shells, fish bones, and skulls of small animals, some gilded and some stained black or purple. These he sold as good-luck charms. For expensive gris gris he had dried bladders of hogs, which he gathered up among the plantations at hog-killing time; for these he charged two dollars and fifty cents. They were used almost exclusively for putting terrible curses upon an individual or his whole family.

There was a Negro, Sol Jefferson, who had been unjustly cursed and struck by the overseer of the plantation where he worked, and being a follower of Charles' cult went to him for means of revenge.

Charles said, "Leave it to me, and do what I say. The moon in the sky is a scientific object, which percolates and simulates according to certain mineral matter exposed to it. Take this bladder, which has been vitalized by the golden rooster and the snake, Zombi, who is in touch with the great spirits of Haiti, fill it with sand from the shores of the great Mississippi, and fling it under the overseer's house on the dot of twelve, midnight. He will wish that he had never struck you, and you will hear from him to that effect."

Sol, half believing, took the bladder, and filled it with sand, as instructed. That night at midnight he threw it under the overseer's house. The next morning he went to work as usual, but did not see his boss. There was another man in his place. Wondering what had happened, and being alarmed, he inquired why the overseer did not come out. A Negro working next to him said, "Ain't you heard? He fell down at fo' o'clock dis monin' and broke his leg."

"That's a lie," cried Sol, forgetting himself, "—it couldn't 'av been that quick."

"What you mean by that?" asked the other Negro, "is you mixed up in it?"

"What makes you ask that?"

"Just what you just said."

"I ain't said nothin'."

"Yes, you is, you just said 'it couldn't be this quick,' and I put two and two together and figured you'd put some gris gris on that man, fo' I knows that you's a friend of Charles the Grinder."

"I sho know 'im," said Sol, "and if you is actin' lak you is, I'm sho' gwine have him put some gris gris on you."

"Lawd, have mercy," cried the Negro, "I don't fool in none o' dat stuff, and you lay off me."

"I sho' will," said Sol, "unless you say something to bring trouble."

The Negro said that was something "I sho' won't do," and Sol was satisfied. But the outcome of the gris gris was very unexpected: Sol did not think it would work at all; and now he had unlimited faith in Charles the Grinder.

Sol did not know, however, that this surprise was nothing compared to what he was later to encounter. The overseer was sent to a hospital in New Orleans, and after several weeks recovered, but he had no sooner reached home when his wife was nearly burnt to death owing to the explosion of a can of kerosene which she used to light a fire in a wood stove, and before she was fully recovered her daughter eloped with a simpleton who had a police record, and as a result of this she nearly lost her mind.

CHARLES THE GRINDER

Sol, being a good man at heart, and thinking that these calamities which befell the overseer's family were results of the hog's bladder filled with sand which he had placed under the house, decided that he had better retrieve it. He waited until the moon was low and the night was dark, and then crept under the house to find the bladder, but could not locate it; he searched for a full hour without success. Meantime the overseer, having heard a noise under his house (for Sol had bumped his head on a rafter several times) decided to take his lantern and gun and go to investigate. As he shined the light on the intruder he thought he recognized Sol, whom he knew very well. "Is that Sol?" he asked.

"No, sir, dis ain't Sol," came the reply.

"Thank goodness," said the overseer, "for I'd hate to shoot Sol."

"Look out, Boss, dis *is* Sol—don't shoot dat gun."

Sol came out from under the house and confessed everything. The overseer was not impressed, however, with the gris gris. "Leave it there," he said, "it can't do any more harm than it's already done."

Sol was relieved and went home happy. But the next day a storm blew the roof off of the overseer's house. Whereupon he sent for Sol and told him to find that bladder or he'd kill him.

Sol found the bladder, and took it home—to his sorrow. He was a middle-aged man, and was married to a very attractive mulatto girl. They had no children. She was very angry with her husband because of his association with Charles the Grinder, and said that she intended to go to see him and give him a "piece of her mind," and get him to move down the river.

Since the bladder was removed from under the overseer's house there was a change in his luck. His wife recovered, and his daughter left the simpleton whom she had married, and returned home, and the owner of the plantation gave him a better house to live in. He had become fond of Sol, and often laughed with him over the "crazy idea" of the gris gris.

Meantime the gris gris was working, not against the overseer, but against Sol himself, now that he had taken it to his own home. His wife had several times gone to see Charles the Grinder, and had become fascinated by his golden rooster, his bones, skulls, and his snake. He told her of his years in Haiti, and of the wonderful life in that country; he told her also of the many countries he had visited while a seaman, and his "big words" interested her; she did not know what they meant—neither did he—but they sounded wonderful; they were not like the "Negro talk" she heard from her husband, and Voodooism, which she once detested, had now become very interesting. She had been asleep; now she was awake, and saw before her a life full of excitement and romance. What had she been doing all these years? Nothing—only getting meals for an ignorant Negro, and that was what she would continue to do; that was all she had to look forward to—living in a cabin, and perhaps never in her lifetime going farther than Baton Rouge—perhaps never as far as New Orleans even. These were the thoughts that Charles the Grinder had put into her innocent head. Her name was Rose-Marie, a pretty name, Charles thought, well suited to a very pretty girl.

The appointed morning came; the house-boat's ropes were pulled in, and it drifted down the current of the Mississippi, never to return, and Rose-Marie was on it with Charles the Grinder. When Sol found his house dark and empty as he returned from work, he suspected, and went to the landing where the boat had been tied up for years. No spot had ever seemed so desolate to him. The boat was gone, and it had carried Rose-Marie away. He knew that. He went home and got the fateful bladder, returned and threw it to the current, hoping that it would curse the river and all that floated on it. But Charles and Rose-Marie were far ahead of it, and they were safe; it would never overtake them. Sol went home, and as he told his story, Voodism became very unpopular in his community.

Gris Gris on His Door-Step Drove Him Mad

Many of the old houses of New Orleans were built close to the sidewalk, and entered by steps, usually of three or four flights. It is today a wonder to strangers why these steps are kept so clean, but that is a time-honored custom; they are scrubbed daily, and sometimes when they are not perfectly clean pulverized brick is spread over them. There has never been any satisfactory explanation for the pulverized brick being spread on perfectly clean steps. The inside of the house can be dusty and grimy, but the steps must be clean, for this gives the public the impression that the whole house is likewise clean. (This is the best explanation I can give of the clean steps of New Orleans; there may be a better one, but I have not heard it.)

There was a man of doubtful morals who had two names, J. D. Rudd and J. B. Langrast. Around 1850 he owned a house on Dumaine Street with a large yard, and there he made his living selling junk, which he stored on the premises, inside the house as well as in the yard. But his steps were always immaculate, and any person entering his quarters was stunned to see the filth—the old clothes, the bed that had not been changed for weeks, and the various items, such as demijohns, broken furniture, cart wheels, and bird cages. But he made considerable money, for half the junk he sold was stolen, and a good portion was given to him. He bought very little. Yet there was not a day he did not make sales amounting to a sum close to a hundred dollars, which in that day was considerable.

The reason he had two names was that he had two wives, one in the uptown section, and one in the downtown section; neither knew of the existence of the other, and as one spoke only French and the other only Spanish they were not likely to meet and compare notes. In the uptown area he was known as Langrast, downtown as Rudd, and when uptown he wore a beautifully tailored suit, and a clean shirt, in fact, dressed like a gentleman, while downtown he wore work clothes, for his wife there, having been bred in a shack, was not very particular. Why he wanted two wives is to this day unexplained, for he spent most of his time at his headquarters-for-junk on Dumaine Street, and slept in a bed hardly fit for animals, much less a man who sometimes dressed like a gentleman and assumed urbane manners. He lived happily in this arrangement for several years, and felt that he was a genius at deception.

A TYPICAL FRONT STEP IN THE OLD NEW ORLEANS

Marie Laveau was at the height of her fame and glory about this time, and was dazzling the people with her incredible achievements, but Langrast hated her and her cult, and all individuals who professed Voodooism. He said they were "the scum of the earth and thieves who would just as soon murder as steal." Whenever there was a mysterious murder in the city he attributed the crime to "some Voodoo." But one morning when he opened his front door he saw on his polished steps a cross and a small bag containing the head of a rooster. This infuriated him, and he started immediately to report the matter to the police, but he had only gone a few blocks when it occurred to him that he was not in a position to invite publicity concerning himself, for he was using two names, and was married to two women. It also occurred to him when his temper had cooled that the police could do little, if anything, about it. The more inconspicuously he lived the better. He turned back, and wondered what he could do with the rooster's head, which he carried with him to show the police, and, being unable to decide, he sauntered into a bar-room and ordered a drink of whiskey. Standing beside him at the bar was a wretched-looking man who seemed to be purposely getting drunk, for he ordered one drink after another.

As Langrast turned to go, this man faced him and said: "You see me? Look at me, I was once a prosperous gentleman. But look at me now. I'm a bum. Why? Would you like to know? It's an interesting story, and I'll tell you. The Voodoos put a curse on me. I was in love with a girl; but that I'll not mention—for reasons better known to myself, sacred reasons, very sacred. The gris gris appeared on my doorstep every morning—every morning—and then my luck began to change. A mockingbird that came and sang at my window every morning vanished; my goldfish died, my dog, Rex, the finest animal that ever lived, was shot, and died in my arms, bidding me farewell, like a human would." Here tears came to his eyes. "I was in the tobacco business, handling perique tobacco grown up here in St. James parish, and I made money; I was on the way to becoming a millionaire, even though I spent money like water."

Langrast did not wish to hear this story, and started out but the man grabbed him by the arm. "Don't be in a hurry; this might happen to you, and I advise you to hear so you can be on guard. My name is John Spiker, and I'm from Kentucky."

Langrast was frightened. It seemed that the gris gris was already working on him. "I'll buy a drink," he said, "and that's all."

As John Spiker waved to the bartender to "bring us two drinks," Langrast slipped the rooster's head into the man's pocket.

The drinks were served, and Spiker began to talk again. "Yes, as I was saying, I kept a carriage, and the best men in the city shook hands with me on the street; but now they don't know me, don't even know my name anymore, don't know my face—as if they'd never seen me. But let me show you my cancelled check for ten thousand, made to cash—pin money—." He reached in his pocket, and as his hand felt the rooster's head his face turned white, and he seemed unable to move a muscle. He turned to see if there was anybody behind him, his hand still in his pocket clutching the rooster's head. Presently he took it out, examined it, and flung it with all his might at the mirror of the bar, breaking two bottles of whiskey.

The bartender went to the rear room of the saloon, and returned with a double-barrelled shot gun, which he pointed toward Langrast and Spiker as he said, "Now, git out o' here, the both of you."

"Why me?" asked Langrast.

"Because I saw you put that rooster's head in Spiker's pocket."

When Spiker heard this he remembered all the curse-words he had ever heard in old Kentucky, and let Langrast have them, swearing that he would kill him if he had a gun, and declaring that if he ever met him when he did have a gun he would lay him low without notice, for this incident simply renewed the curse which had been placed upon him, prolonging it—"no telling how long."

THE IDOL MAKER

The bartender, having cooled down, put his gun away, and having enjoyed Spiker's magnificent cursing, said that the boys could have a drink on the house, and to show them that gris gris meant nothing to him he would preserve the rooster's head in a glass of his best whiskey and keep it on the liquor stand.

Spiker stood still for a moment; then, with fresh tears running down his cheeks, shook hands with Langrast. Having enjoyed the drink on the house, they decided that they would get drunk together, and they swore that they would "clean up Voodooism in New Orleans," and expose it "as the dirtiest racket that ever existed or go back to a civilized country, either Tennessee or Kentucky, where a man would shoot you face to face, but wouldn't stoop to putting gris gris on your door-step and causing your death by slow humiliation and starvation."

They nearly drank the bar-room dry, at Langrast's expense, for he was prosperous. Sometime in the early morning they staggered homeward, and when Langrast reached his house he saw a fresh cross and another rooster's head on his steps. This drove him mad. He went into his house, took his shotgun, and began shooting the steps away, at the same time cursing the Voodoos and swearing that he would kill the last one "infesting this city." The neighbors called the police, and Langrast was lodged in jail.

When he was released, after paying a heavy fine, he sold his business for a song, deserted both of his wives and left the city.

Thirty years later an old man arrived in New Orleans from Peru, and registered at the St. Louis Hotel as J. B. Langrast. He spoke Spanish fluently, and was very wealthy, for he caused a sensation in banking circles by depositing half a million in a New Orleans bank. After a while he began to search for Mrs. J. D. Rudd and Mrs. J. B. Langrast. He found that Mrs. Rudd was dead, and Mrs. Langrast, now fifty, was working as a waitress in the St. Louis Hotel. He went into the restaurant and recognized her. But she did not recognize him; he had grown very old, and since he had nearly forgotten the English language she could not recall his voice—his intonation had changed. But he finally convinced her that he was her husband, and took her with him to Tennessee, which to him was a civilized country wherein he wished to spend the rest of his life—where a man never shot you in the back, nor tortured you with gris gris and put a curse on you.

TELLING YOUR FUTURE IS FOREVER FASCINATING
"You Will Marry a Rich Man."
Leslie's Weekly — 1898

PALMISTRY IS ONE OF THE OLDEST OF PREDICTIVE SYSTEMS

The following is from GLEASON'S PICTORIAL — 1885

DIVINATION—the prediction of future events from some present data—has ever found many credulous believers. No nation has ever been chronicled by the pen of the historian, either in ancient or in modern days, in which superstitious people did not give evidence to some system of divination. The Greeks and the Romans had their oracles; the Indians of our western prairies have their sorcerers; and in every Christian city at the present time may be found professional "fortune-tellers." Divination flourishes in the very ages in which reason most prevails over feeling; and, strange to say, many eminent men, who have risen far above the prejudices of their age, and have even disregarded important truths, have given themselves up to superstitious trust in some species of prediction. The ancient Germans had consecrated white horses, from whose snorting or neighing they drew favorable or unfavorable signs. The Greek oracle of Apollo, at Delphi, on the side of Mount Parnassus, was interpreted by a Pythonisa, or fair priestess, who sat over the sacred cavity on a golden tripod, and inhaled the mystic vapor until she became inspired. At Antium, there were statues of Fortune, who responded to questions propounded by moving their heads, and Egypt yet retains the vast structures used by her divinatory. At more recent dates, astrology was implicitly believed in by those who looked confidently into futurity, but within the past century, *chiromancy* has been the popular "medium." Basing their belief on texts in Job and Solomon, the believers in chiromancy cite many a "proof" of the truthfulness of their science, and refer with triumph to the famous Madame Le Normand, who exercised such an influence over Napoleon and the ill-starred Josephine. Of course, we do not think to impose this system upon the readers of the Pictorial, whose good sense would repel any serious attempts to excite their superstitions by attempting to unveil the mysteries of futurity. But having obtained from France drawings of the "system" which governed Madame Le Normand, we have thought it might he amusing to many, and be a novel pastime at social gatherings. There is surely no more impropriety in divining character, or the paths of life in which one's peculiar disposition will lead them by the hand than by the head, and we submit the "charts," as a novel amusement, stripped of the mystic apparatus with which professional divinators surround themselves, as may be seen in the design at the head of this article. The old astrologer, clothed in his professional uniform, and surrounded by the hideous and mystical insignia of his art, was often the terror of princes, and earnestly did they invoke him to read their horoscopes. Astronomical instruments, books filled with cabalistic signs, crosset-lamps and hour-glasses, imposed upon the ignorant of the dark ages, even as in these enlightened times, when scores flock to some keen-witted old dame, generally to seek information about their lover, they gaze with superstitious reverence at her cat, her raven, and her oracular cards. A truce to such pretensions; and if any one wishes to enjoy the joke of chiromancy—the most favorite scheme of divination—here is the entire key and mystery.

LINES.—There are five important "lines," most of which are to be found upon the right hand of every one, and which indicate certain results, viz.:—*The Line of Life*, 1-2. In persons destined to a ripe old age, this line is clearly marked, and distinctly traced. Faint breaks or ramifications, indicate illness, or accident, and if it increases in distinctness as it approaches the wrist, it foretells a healthy, vigorous old age. *The Line of Intellect*, 1-3. Those who concentrate their talents upon one subject, have a well-traced line across the hand in this direction, while in others more diversified and varied in their mental pursuits, it branches off. Depth of color and distinctness indicate the quantity of mental ability which the lines denote. *The Line of Happiness*, 4-5. Those who live in "peace and good will" have this line distinctly marked, and will ever enjoy the tranquil happiness attendant upon a quiet life. When this happiness is promoted by a love of various pursuits, the line branches off as it approaches 5, but those who have but "one idea," have but a single trace. *The Line of Love*, 4-9. This line denotes a warm, devoted heart, capable of bestowing and of receiving affection. Those destined to lead a single life never possess it, and its depth of color, distinctness and unity, are so many indexes to the heart of its possessor. *The Line of Trouble*, 9-6. Those who, from an impetuous or vicious disposition, are prone to trouble, have this line clearly across the palm. *The Line of Fortune*, 9—8. This line, when clear and distinct, indicates the power of accumulating and keeping wealth. *The Heart Centre*, 6. Lines springing from this spot to any other termination, or joining any other line, show that the possessor has any given trait so identified in a high sense. *The Line of Jointure*, 7-2. This line, or oftener these lines, indicate future inheritances, the extent of which is foreshadowed by the breadth and color of the lines.

MOUNTAINS.—The small risings on the hand are termed "mountains," and indicate the present character of their possessor, viz.:— *Mountain of Venus*, A. When full and clear—true, steadfast and reliable. Furrowed by lines—variable and fickle. Spotted—false and treacherous. Dark-colored—jealous and revengeful. *Mountain of Jupiter*, B. This, well developed, indicates industry, application and energy. When crossed by two rays, the possessor is prone to extravagance. *Mountain of Saturn*, C. When rounded off evenly, this indicates a gentle disposition; but if colored, it is a sign of melancholy and sadness. *Mountain of Mars*, D. This, when clearly developed, denotes true courage, and bravery guided by prudence. When of a high color, it indicates audacity and temerity, but the want of it, or a slight development of it, is a sure token of weakness and indecision. *Mountain of Mercury*, E. Situated at the commencement of the little finger, this protuberance is an important index to the possessor's character. When clear and distinct, it denotes constancy in the affections, and fidelity in promises. If intersected by a wrinkle, the person can easily be swerved from the path of duty, or diverted from the object of his affection, while a perpendicular "line," forming with the horizontal wrinkle a cross, indicates a firm religious belief, not easily shaken. *Mountain of the Moon*, 7-3. This development along the lower edge of the hand, indicates a fondness for theatrical amusements, music, or singing, and is very prominent on the hands of orators. The *Hollow of the Hand*, if deep and regularly formed, indicates happiness and long life.

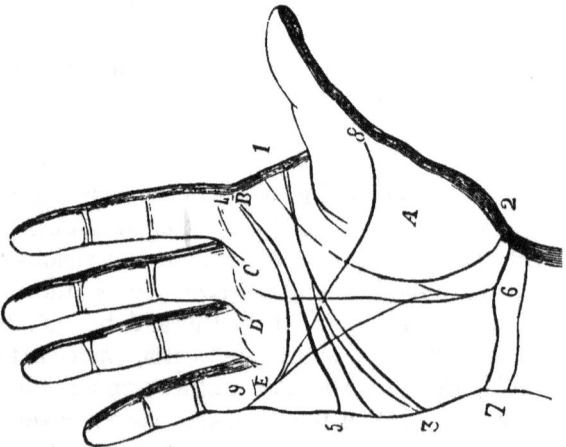

The "*Trace of Disappointment*" (below) surrounds the "Mountain of Saturn," and denotes some disappointment in affairs of the heart, which cannot be effaced. Occasionally, there is a double line, but the first is the deepest and most endurable.

There are other "lines" which indicate particular events. "*Nuptial Line*" (next page), from the commencement of the thumb, parallel with the "line of life," betokens marriage and happiness, the duration of which is indicated by the length of the "nuptial line."

The *"Line of Joy"* (below), extends from the base of the thumb directly across the hand, mid is not permanent, lint appears to herald any event calculated to gladden the heart of the possessor. It is not indented as other "lines" are, but traced as it were.

The *"Line of Professional Success"* (below) starts from the commencement of the thumb, and runs parallel with the "line of intellect," just below it. If it crosses the "line of fortune," it betokens a lucrative reward for study and toil early in life.

The *"Line of Travel"* (next page) is a small trace which strikes into the "line of life," forming a triangle. It indicates that the possessor will soon go on a journey, the length of which is indicated by the acuteness of the apex, that expands with the distance.

The "*Trace of Indecision*" (below), which surrounds the "Mountain of Mars," shows that the possessor has neglected one of those golden opportunities which secure fortune, fame, and happiness—and which, once passed, cannot be regained.

The "*Line of Success*" (below), nearly encircles the thumb, just above its departure from the hand; and two lines above it indicate a happy accomplishment of the plans nearest the heart—one "line" promising hope, but not warranting perfect confidence.

The "*Line of Hymen*" (next page), is a trace that comes around the "Mountain of Saturn," and crosses the hand, nearly parallel with the "line of happiness." It promises marriage, and that speedy if it comes upwards towards its centre.

The *"Trace of Evil"* (below), encircles the "Mountain of Mercury," and is the stamp of wrong, although the possessor may have been a victim to the evil enticements of others. It is seldom found in the gentler sex.

JACK TINPAN AND THE GHOST AT HOLLINS' GATE

When I was a boy my family lived on a plantation on the Mississippi River, and had a yardman, Jack Tinpan, who spent most of his time telling ghost stories. His stories thrilled you to the bones. If he had been an educated man he could have made a respectable sum of money writing these weird accounts of ghosts he saw, with a touch of humor in them. Jack had been in our family all his life; he was, in fact, born on our place, and was my grandfather's favorite slave, who had only to saddle the horses, open the gates, and, on occasions, serve juleps. He never put in a hard day's work in his life. But he always complained at the end of the day he was "burnt out," and that was why in the evenings he needed a flask of whiskey to keep him going until bedtime.

He lived always alone in a shack on the place, and that is where the ghosts visited him. They carried lanterns until they reached his shack, then put them out so their voices in the darkness would frighten him all the more. These visitations were after he had gone to bed, and he pulled the covers over his head, refusing to hear, but their voices were so loud they reached his ears through the covers. So he said. They told him that the levee would break when the next high water came, but our house would not float away, for he, Jack Tinpan, would be there to tie it to an oak tree that stood nearby; that he was going to have an accident unless he kept away from plows and cultivators; that Aunt Ann, who was our cook, was going to the devil unless she quit lying, stealing, and whipping her grandchild, whose name, by the way, was "Ten-cents." What the ghosts told him would fill several volumes. (Aunt Ann, let me explain, was a very honest woman, but Jack Tinpan didn't like her.)

There was a farmer, Herman Hollins, whose farm was next to our place, and who, according to Jack Tinpan, was a cruel man, who stabbed out the eyes of his hogs that had the habit of eating young chickens; and when one of his mules became unruly he knocked it unconscious with a club, which he carried with him for the purpose. The Negroes on our place and the surrounding plantations were deathly afraid of him. That is what Jack told me. I relied upon him solely for the gossip and horror stories of the neighborhood. He supplied them in abundance.

Mr. Hollins, as I recall him, was a queer man. He wore a long beard and seldom spoke to me; and as a matter of fact, I never got very close to him, for I was awed by his beard, which never seemed very clean. The fact that he wore a blue flannel shirt winter and summer, and never a white linen shirt, not even on Sundays, set him aside, in my opinion, as a man who did not belong to the community. That is all I remember of Mr. Hollins, except that one day he died, and there were very few people who attended his funeral. My family ignored it, and this surprised me. I recall that I asked Jack Tinpan why he was not getting us ready to go.

"Because nobody ain't going," he replied.

"Why?" I asked, knowing that my father attended every funeral in the community.

"Mr. Hollins didn't have no friends, 'cept the devil," he answered, "and only the devil knew him."

"Why?" I asked again. "Was it only because he was cruel to animals? Was he cruel to human beings, too?"

"No," said Jack Tinpan, "he never hit no human beings, 'cause a human being can hit back, but a poor animal can't. But we ain't done with him yet; his ghost will be around my shack. The animals, they can't hear nor see no ghost, and they'll be free."

After Mr. Hollins was buried and forgotten, Jack Tinpan asked me to accompany him to his shack one evening, for he had something to tell me. As soon as he had his supper, which he always ate in our kitchen, I followed him, expecting a thrilling story. He took a drink of whiskey, and gave me a bench to sit on.

"What have you seen?" I asked eagerly.

'There's something that's been going on for some time," he said. "Every night at twelve o'clock on the dot of the hour, Mr. Hollins' ghost opens and closes that front gate to the Hollins' farm—invisible-like."

"Who saw it?" I asked.

"Well, I seen it for ten nights straight," he replied. "It never misses—just as sure as midnight comes that gate opens."

"Are you the only person who saw it?" I inquired.

"No, I ain't," he said. "Gus Adams has seen it. You can ask him."

"Why does Mr. Hollins' ghost do that?," I wanted to know.

"There ain't no trouble in answering that," said Jack Tinpan, as he pulled a flask of whiskey from his back pocket and took another drink; "it just for cussed meanness; for the same reason he hit those poor animals."

Since I never stayed up until midnight this did not concern me very much. But the next day when I saw Gus Adams in the yard (he was a field worker, and did not have the ease and leisure of Jack Tinpan), I asked him if he knew about the gate.

"Sho' do," he said. "Ain't Jack Tinpan told you?"

"Yes," I replied, "but he tells so many crazy ghost stories I can't believe all he says."

"That's sho' true," agreed Gus Adams, "you can't believe that man, for he's sho' the biggest liar on this side o' Hell. But every night that gate opens and closes invisible-like. But there's something Jack Tinpan ain't seen, and I don't aim to tell 'im. Every Saturday night at the old Hollins' well a light flutters on the ground, and around it rolls a skull with a long beard attached. When that light's there you can see an owl in the tree."

Gus Adams was a reliable man, who attended church regularly and did not drink. He was convincing, and I believed that the gate opened and closed at midnight on the dot, but I did not believe that the light came by the well nor that an owl was always in the tree at the same time. In fact, if he had only confirmed Jack Tinpan's story about the gate, I would have believed him implicitly, but since I could not believe the story about the skull, the light, and the owl I had some doubts also about the gate.

For some reason I did not tell my father about this. I think it was because I felt sure that if I did, he would caution Jack Tinpan about telling me ghost stories; then there would not be no more stories that thrilled.

Anyway, a year passed by, and I was invited to a party at the house of a friend who lived several miles away. Jack Tinpan saddled my horse, and away I went. I had forgotten about Hollins' gate. But the party lasted until nearly midnight, and I started home. The moon was bright and it never occurred to me to be fearful; but when I approached the Hollins' gate I suddenly remembered the story, and I took out my watch to see the time by the moonlight. It was exactly one minute to twelve. A minute was to seem like a century, and with chills running up and down my spine I stopped my horse to wait for the hour hand to reach twelve. The gate was closed. I had not decided in that minute what I would do if it opened. I felt some consolation, I recall, in the fact that Jack Tinpan had assured me Hollins' ghost made itself invisible on this occasion. At least I would only see the movement of the gate.

The hand of my watch reached twelve. Despite my fear, I wished that the gate would open, for that would be at least an exciting experience. I waited. The gate did not open. It did not move, but stood as still as the Pyramids. It was not going to open; I knew that, but I stood there for three minutes longer, growing braver and braver. In fact, I was so very brave now that I ardently wished the gate to open. The air was still; there was not even a breeze to stir the leaves on the trees and the bushes near the gate.

Convinced that I was a person of unusual courage, and that Jack Tinpan was a fake, I beckoned my horse to proceed.

When I reached our own gate, which was about a hundred yards up the road, I found, to my surprise, that it was open. As I drew near, it closed of its own accord! Something invisible had closed it. All my courage left me. It seemed as if my hair stood straight and I was sure that it had suddenly turned white, for I had just been memorizing THE PRISONER OF CHILLON —

> "My hair is gray, but not from years,
> Nor grew it white
> In a single night
> As man's have grown from sudden fears."

If I had thought (but I was unable to) I would have gone a few yards ahead and taken the lane leading to the Negro quarters, but I instantly got off my horse and pulled the gate open again.

When I did so I found a black dog which, formerly tied to the stake in the Negro quarters, had pulled away, taking the stake and chain with him, and made his way to our gate in which he became entangled. When he saw me he attempted to get away and in doing so he pulled the gate and closed it.

When I reached the smaller yard surrounding our residence, I hurriedly took the saddle and bridle off my horse, threw them on the ground, and rushed into the house. I looked in the first mirror I came upon to see if my hair was white. Not a white strand could I see.

The next morning when I saw Jack Tinpan he asked me why I had not unsaddled my horse at the stable.

"That is my business," I said. "But please do not tell me any more ghost stories, for I will not believe them. You said that the Hollins' gate would open at midnight. I passed there at midnight and nothing happened."

"Well," he said, "the reason Mr. Hollins' ghost ain't been at that gate is because it was on my roof taking the bricks off the chimney. Come and see."

When I reached the shack I saw that about a dozen bricks had fallen from his chimney, but I knew that the structure was more than a hundred years old, and it could easily be falling to pieces.

The fact is that Jack Tinpan had lost his art or I had simply outgrown it. His tales did not thrill me any longer. He had become childish. I had become a man. He settled down, ate well, drank more and more, stopped work altogether, and lived to be a hundred. My people took very good care of him to the last day of his life. They moved him into a brick house, gave him ample food, clothes to wear, whiskey to drink, and all the tobacco he could use.

Bibliography

The Louisiana Historical Quarterly
The New-Orleans City Guide
Psychical Research and the Resurrection—James H. Hyslop, Ph.D., LL.D.
Encyclopedia Britannica
Voodoo in New Orleans—Robert Tallant
Black Odyssey—Roi Ottley
The Science of Life—H. G. Wells
Slavery in the Roman Empire—R. H. Barrow, M.A., B.Litt.
Abnormal Psychology—Isador H. Coriat, M.D.
The Negro: The Southerner's Problem—Thomas Nelson Page
The Times Democrat
The Picayune
Century Magazine—George W. Cable
A Paper by Thomas H. Furlong (in New Orleans Public Library)
Memoirs of Louis XIV and His Regency—Duke of Saint-Simon
The Magic Island—W. B. Seabrook
The White King of La Gonave—Faustin Wirkus & Taney Dudley
American Standard Encyclopedia—L. Colange, LL.D.
Great Events by Famous Historians
Santo Domingo, Past & Present—Samuel Hazard
Library of Southern Literature—E. A. Alderman, J. C. Harris and C. W. Kent
The Land Columbus Loved—Bertita Harding
The Journey Toward the Sunlight—Stanley Walker
Familiar Quotations—John Bartlett
Critical & Historical Essays—Thomas Babington Macaulay
Aesop's Fables—G. K. Chesterton

Visit us at *www.quaintpress.com*.

www.ingramcontent.com/pod-product-compliance
Lightning Source LLC
Chambersburg PA
CBHW070524100426
42743CB00010B/1944